MOHSIN ALI

SALES MASTERY

Practical Techniques to Close Deals Like A CURRENT TOP SALE EXPERT

Contents

1

Dedication

To all the entrepreneurs out there—
the dreamers, the risk-takers, and the relentless doers.
This book is for those who dare to turn ideas into reality,
who face challenges head-on and never give up.
May it inspire you to reach new heights and master the art of sales.
This journey is yours—keep pushing forward.

2

The Proven ALEX HARMOZI Shortcut To Mastering Sales Conversations

I f you've ever found yourself lost in the sea of sales advice out there, you're not alone. I've been there too—spending countless hours watching videos, reading articles, and taking notes, all in search of the best strategies to close more deals.

One name that kept coming up was **Alex Hormozi**, a master of sales psychology and closing techniques. So, I did the hard work for you. I watched all of **Alex Hormozi's sales videos,** dissected every strategy, and distilled them into clear, actionable steps.

This book is your shortcut. You won't have to spend hours watching video after video, trying to pick out the golden nuggets. Instead, you'll find the most powerful strategies and techniques laid out for you, step by step, in a way that's easy to understand and put into practice.

You'll learn how to turn sales calls into meaningful conversations that build trust, solve problems, and leave your prospects feeling excited to work with you. Whether you're just starting in sales or looking to sharpen your skills, this book will equip you with everything you need to succeed.

Let's get started on transforming the way you approach sales—saving you time, frustration, and leading you to close more deals, faster.

The Purpose of This Book

In this book, we're going to learn some of Alex Hormozi's best sales techniques. But don't worry—you won't need a business degree or a lot of experience to understand them. We're going to keep it simple, fun, and full of examples that anyone can understand (yes, even third graders!).

Here's what we're going to cover:

- **How to overcome objections**: When someone says, "I'm not sure," or "It's too expensive," you'll know exactly what to say to help them feel confident in their decision.
- **How to close deals**: We'll show you how to turn "maybe" into "yes" so that people feel excited to buy from you.

What You'll Learn in This Book

By the time you finish reading this book, you'll have a box of tools that you can use anytime you need to persuade someone or make a sale. You'll learn how to:

- **Understand what people really want**: So you can show them how your product or idea can help them.
- **Handle objections and concerns**: So you can turn "no" into "yes" without being pushy.

3

The Promise of This Book

I promise that by the end of this book, you will have the skills and confidence to overcome objections and close more deals. You'll learn how to turn "no" into "yes," help people make decisions they feel good about.

Whether you're selling something now or dreaming of starting your own business one day, these sales techniques will help you succeed. So, let's get started and learn how to become amazing at sales, just like Alex Hormozi!

Are you ready? Let's go!

4

Selling with Logic and Emotion

Why Selling with Both Logic and Emotion Matters
Imagine you're shopping for a new car. At first, you're drawn to a sleek, red sports car because it excites you. But then, you consider the car's fuel efficiency, safety ratings, and reliability. This mix of **emotion and logic** is what ultimately drives your purchase decision.

In sales, appealing to both the emotional and rational sides of a client is essential. While emotions often ignite the initial interest, **logic provides the reassurance** clients need to commit and stay satisfied with their purchase. This chapter will explore how to balance these two elements to create a compelling and trustworthy sales process.

Three Strategies for Selling with Both Logic and Emotion

Engaging clients on both an emotional and logical level can help you close deals more effectively and reduce buyer's remorse. Here's how you can achieve that balance to build strong, lasting client relationships.

1. Engage Emotions to Spark Interest

Emotions are powerful motivators. They drive clients to explore options, dream of new possibilities, and take action. Tapping into your client's emotional triggers can create excitement and urgency around your product or service.

How to Appeal to Emotions

- **Tell Compelling Stories**: Share client success stories that show how your service has transformed lives or businesses. Use relatable scenarios to evoke feelings of hope, excitement, or relief.
- **Use Visual Imagery**: Incorporate images, videos, or vivid language that helps clients visualise the benefits they'll experience. "Imagine waking up every morning feeling energised and ready to take on the day."
- **Tap into Aspirations**: Connect with your clients' dreams and desires. For example, "This program isn't just about making more money; it's about giving you the freedom to live life on your terms."

Example: Imagine you're selling a weight loss coaching program.

- **You**: "Imagine how amazing you'll feel when you reach your fitness goals—more energy, confidence, and the ability to wear whatever you want."

Tip: Use emotion to highlight the impact of your product on your client's life, not just the product's features.

2.Provide Logical Justifications to Build Confidence

While emotions initiate the purchase, clients often need logical reassurance to commit fully. By addressing practical concerns and providing evidence of value, you help clients feel secure in their decision.

How to Appeal to Logic

- **Break Down ROI**: Show clients the tangible benefits they'll receive. For example, explain how a one-time investment in your program can lead to increased revenue or time saved.
- **Use Data and Testimonials**: Share statistics, case studies, and testimonials that back up your claims. "Our clients see an average of 30% growth in their business within the first six months."
- **Address Concerns Upfront**: Tackle common objections head-on. If clients are worried about the cost, break down the value over time. "This program costs $1,000, but it's designed to save you $5,000 in expenses over the next year."

Example: Imagine you're selling a business consulting service.

- **Client**: "It seems expensive."
- **You**: "I understand. But let's break it down: if you invest $5,000 in this service, we'll help you increase your revenue by at least $20,000 over the next year. That's a 4x return on your investment."

Tip: Use logic to demonstrate the long-term benefits and value of your product, reducing the risk of buyer's remorse.

3. Combine Emotion and Logic in Your Sales Conversations

A balanced approach of appealing to both emotions and logic can turn hesitant prospects into enthusiastic buyers. Start with emotional appeals to capture interest, then provide logical reasons to solidify their decision.

How to Combine Emotion and Logic

- **Start with Emotion**: Engage clients by focusing on their dreams, goals, and challenges. "I can see how much you want to achieve [desired outcome], and this program is designed to help you get there."
- **Transition to Logic**: Once they're emotionally invested, provide the logical evidence they need to feel confident in their decision. "Let me show you how this program delivers results with proven strategies and measurable outcomes."
- **Close with a Blend**: Reinforce both the emotional and logical benefits. "Not only will this program help you achieve your goals, but it's also a smart investment that will pay off in the long run."

Example: Imagine you're selling an online course to help clients build passive income.

- **You**: "Imagine the freedom of having consistent passive income so you can spend more time with your family. Plus, with our step-by-step system, you'll see results within six months—saving you years of trial and error."
- **Tip**: Use stories and data together to create a persuasive, well-rounded argument that appeals to both the heart and the mind.

Why These Strategies Work

Clients need both emotional motivation and logical justification to feel secure in their purchase decisions. By effectively blending these two approaches, you create a sales process that not only attracts clients but also keeps them satisfied long after the purchase.

Key Benefits:

1. **Reduces Buyer's Remorse**: Logical justifications help clients feel confident about their purchase, reducing regret.
2. **Increases Client Commitment**: Clients who are both emotionally and logically invested are more likely to stick with your program and achieve their goals.
3. **Improves Closing Rates**: Engaging both the emotional and rational sides of clients increases your chances of closing deals successfully.

Action Step: For your next sales call, prepare a story that appeals to emotions and a data-driven fact that appeals to logic. Use both to address client concerns and close the deal.

Key Takeaways

1. **Engage Emotions First**: Capture clients' interest by tapping into their desires, dreams, and challenges.
2. **Reinforce with Logic**: Provide data, ROI breakdowns, and evidence to reassure clients of the value of their investment.
3. **Blend Emotion and Logic**: Use a balanced approach to turn interest into commitment and long-term satisfaction.

End of Chapter Challenge

Here's your challenge: For your next three sales interactions, use both an emotional appeal and a logical argument to address client concerns. Note how it influences their decision-making process and their confidence in committing to your service.

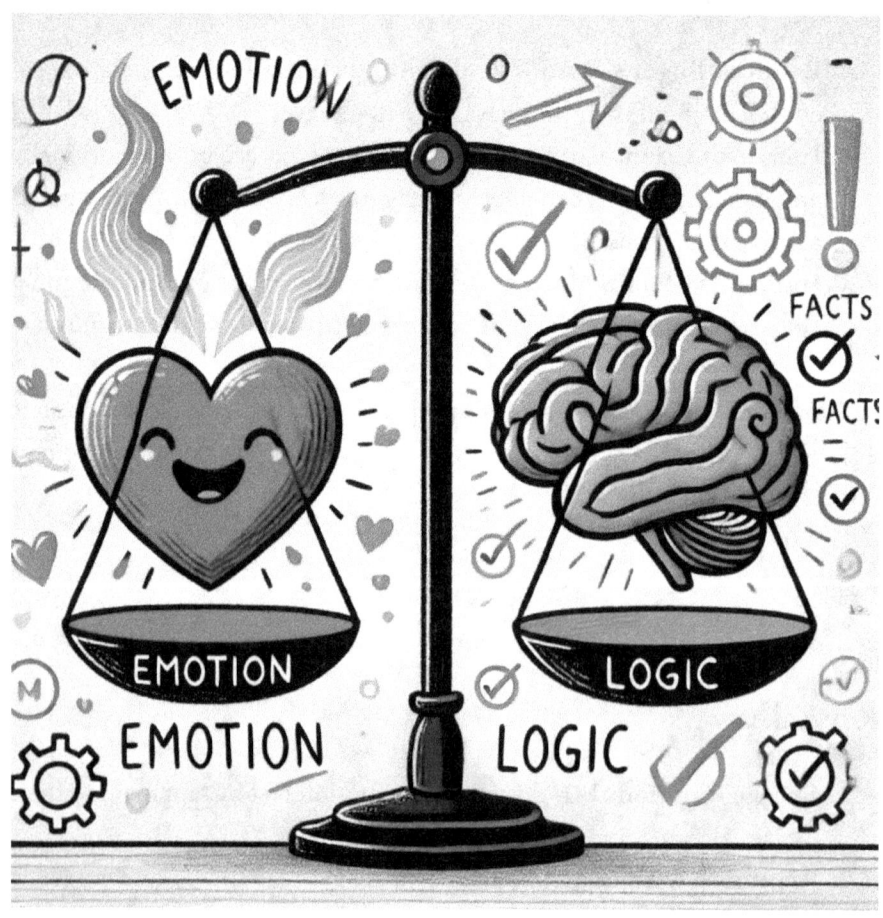

5

Building Trust and Conviction – The Secret to Consistent Sales Success

What is Conviction and Why is it So Important?

Imagine you're trying to convince your friend to watch your favourite movie. If you're excited, confident, and sure that it's the best movie ever, your friend will probably get excited too. But if you're unsure and say, "Well, I think it's okay, but you might not like it," your friend probably won't be interested.

In sales, **conviction** means truly believing in what you're selling. If you are confident and enthusiastic about your product, that feeling is contagious! The person you're talking to will start to feel excited and confident too. But if you seem unsure or hesitant, they'll pick up on that and start doubting whether they should buy.

How Conviction Builds Trust with Your Customers

People can tell if you truly believe in what you're saying. When they see that you're confident and passionate, they trust you more. And when customers trust you, they're much more likely to buy from you.

Example: Imagine you're trying to sell a new pair of running shoes to a friend. If you say, "These are the best running shoes I've ever worn! They're super comfortable, and they help me run faster," your friend will be excited to try them. But if you say, "Well, I think they're good, but I'm not really sure," your friend won't be as interested.

How Conviction Affects Your Sales Streaks

In sales, there are times when everything seems easy, and you're closing deals left and right. These are called **hot streaks**. But sometimes, it feels like no one wants to buy, no matter what you do. These are **cold streaks**.

Here's the secret: these streaks are often connected to how much you believe in what you're selling. If you start doubting your product after a tough conversation with a customer, that doubt can sneak into your next sales calls. When you don't believe in what you're selling, your customers won't either.

Example: Imagine you're trying to sell tickets to a school play. At first, you're super excited, and you sell lots of tickets. But then one person tells you, "I don't think it's worth it." You start to feel unsure, and suddenly, it becomes harder to sell more tickets because you've lost some of your excitement.

How to Regain Your Conviction When You're in a Cold Streak

If you're feeling unsure or having a hard time making sales, don't worry! There are ways to get your confidence back:

1. Remind Yourself of Past Successes

One of the best ways to rebuild your conviction is to look back at your past wins. Think about the times when customers were really happy with your product.

- **Action**: Watch recordings of successful sales calls or read positive reviews from happy customers. This will remind you why your product is valuable and why people love it.

Example: If you're selling homemade crafts and feeling discouraged, look at the messages from customers who said how much they loved your work. It will help you feel proud and excited again.

2. Focus on the Benefits of Your Product

Sometimes, it's easy to forget all the good things your product can do for people, especially if you've had a rough day. Take a moment to remind yourself why your product is special.

- **Action**: Write down the top 3 benefits of your product. For example, if you're selling a study guide, remind yourself that it helps students get better grades and feel more confident in school.

3. Practice Talking About Your Product with Enthusiasm

If you're feeling unsure, practise talking about your product to a friend or even in front of a mirror. The more you talk about it, the more excited you'll feel.

- **Action**: Try to remember why you fell in love with the product in the first place. When you share that excitement, others will feel it too.

How to Transfer Your Conviction to Your Customers

Once you've rebuilt your confidence, it's time to pass that belief onto your customers. Here are some easy ways to do that:

1. Speak with Confidence and Energy

Imagine you're trying to convince your friend to join your soccer team. If you say, "It's so much fun, and we get to play every weekend!" with a big smile on your face, your friend will feel excited too. But if you say it in a dull voice, they won't feel as enthusiastic.

Tip: Use your voice, your facial expressions, and even your hands to show how much you believe in what you're selling. Enthusiasm is contagious!

2. Share Success Stories

Sometimes, customers need a little proof that your product works. Sharing stories of other happy customers can help them believe in your product too.

- **Example**: If you're selling an online course, tell your potential customer about another student who used the course and improved their grades.

3. Use Positive Language

Instead of saying, "I think this might help you," say, "I'm confident this will help you." Words like "believe," "know," and "sure" can make a big difference.

Key Takeaways

1. **Conviction is contagious**: When you believe in your product, your customers will too.
2. **Confidence builds trust**: If you're confident, your customers will trust you and feel more comfortable buying.
3. **Regain your belief by focusing on past successes**: Remind yourself of the good things your product does and the happy customers you've helped.

Action Step: Take a moment to write down three things you love about your product. Then, practise talking about those things with excitement to a friend or family member.

End of Chapter Challenge

Here's a fun challenge: The next time you're trying to sell something, focus on speaking with enthusiasm and confidence. Try to transfer your excitement to the person you're talking to. Afterward, think about how it went. Did they seem more interested?

6

Handling Objections and Embracing "No" Responses

Why "No" is Not the End—It's Just the Beginning
Imagine you're trying to invite your friend to play at your house. You ask, "Do you want to come over and play video games?" But your friend says, "No, I have homework." How do you feel? Maybe you feel a little disappointed, but here's the thing: that "no" isn't the end. It's actually the beginning of figuring out how to change their mind.

In sales, hearing "no" is totally normal. It doesn't mean you've failed. It just means there's something your customer is worried about, and it's your job to find out what that is and help them feel better about saying "yes."

Why You Should Expect "No" Responses

When you're trying to sell something, it's important to remember that most people won't say "yes" right away. They might have concerns, questions, or worries. But that's okay! If customers could easily make decisions on their own, they wouldn't need you to guide them.

Example: Imagine you're trying to sell tickets to your school's charity event. When you ask your neighbour if they'd like to buy a ticket, they say, "No, I don't think I can go." Instead of giving up, you can ask, "What's stopping you? Is it because you're busy, or is there something else?"

By expecting that people might say "no" at first, you can plan how to respond and help them see the value of what you're offering.

The Mindset Shift: Turning "No" into an Opportunity

One of the most important lessons in sales is to stop being afraid of hearing "no." Instead, think of it like a game. When someone says "no," it's just a clue that you need to dig deeper to understand their concerns.

Here's a little secret: Most of the time, "no" doesn't mean they're not interested. It just means they need more information or reassurance. Maybe they're worried about the price, the time commitment, or whether they really need what you're selling.

Action Tip: The next time someone says "no," don't get discouraged. Instead, see it as a chance to ask questions and learn more about what they need.

How to Handle "No" Like a Pro

Let's break down a few ways to handle objections and turn "no" into "yes":

1. Ask Open-Ended Questions

If someone says, "No, I'm not interested," don't just walk away. Try to find out why. Ask questions that can't be answered with a simple "yes" or "no." This helps you understand their real concerns.

- **Example**: If you're trying to sell a drawing class and the customer says, "No, I'm too busy," you can ask, "I understand you're busy—what's the biggest thing taking up your time right now?" This helps you see if there's a way to fit your class into their schedule.

2. Show Empathy and Understand Their Concerns

When someone says "no," it's often because they have worries or doubts. Instead of pushing harder, take a moment to show that you understand.

- **Example**: If a customer says, "No, I can't afford it," you can respond, "I totally understand. It's important to be careful with money. But what if I told you this product could save you money in the long run?"

Tip: When people feel understood, they're more likely to open up and share what's really bothering them.

Training Example: Role-Playing to Overcome Objections

Imagine you're training new salespeople. One of the best ways to help them get comfortable with objections is through **role-playing**. This is like pretending to be in a real-life sales conversation so that they can practise how to handle "no" responses.

How to Run a Role-Playing Exercise

1. **Set up a scenario**: Let's say the salesperson is trying to sell a fitness program. The customer (played by a trainee) starts by saying, "No, I'm not sure if this program is right for me."

2. **Guide the trainee to ask questions**: Teach them to respond with, "I understand. What's holding you back? Is it the time commitment, the cost, or something else?"
3. **Encourage exploring concerns**: If the customer says, "I'm not sure if I'll have the time," the trainee can practice responding with, "That's totally understandable. But what if I told you it only takes 10 minutes a day? Would that fit better into your schedule?"

By practising how to handle objections in a safe environment, new salespeople can build confidence. They learn to see "no" not as a rejection but as a chance to understand the customer better.

Embracing "No" as Part of the Process

Imagine you're playing a video game, and every time you reach a tricky level, you get frustrated and quit. You'd never

finish the game, right? But if you see those tricky parts as challenges to beat, you'll feel excited to keep trying.

In sales, "no" is like those tricky levels. It's just a part of the game, and every "no" gets you one step closer to a "yes."

Key Tip: The more you practise handling objections, the better you'll get at turning "no" into "yes." Soon, it will start to feel like a fun challenge rather than something to be afraid of.

Key Takeaways

1. **Expect "no" responses**: It's normal! Use them as opportunities to understand what the customer really needs.
2. **Ask questions to uncover concerns**: Don't be afraid to ask, "What's holding you back?" It can lead to valuable conversations.
3. **Practice makes perfect**: Role-playing with friends or coworkers can help you get better at handling objections.

Action Step: The next time someone says "no" to something you're offering, don't give up. Try asking, "What's the biggest concern you have right now?" Practise this with a friend to get comfortable with handling objections.

End of Chapter Challenge

Here's your challenge: Find a friend or family member and practise a role-play scenario where they say "no" to something you're trying to sell. See if you can turn that "no" into a "yes" by asking questions and addressing their concerns. Remember, every "no" is just one step closer to a "yes"!

7

Selling as the First Step in Coaching

Why Selling is More Than Just Making a Sale

I magine you're convincing your friend to join your soccer team. You're not just trying to get them to sign up—you want them to have fun, get better at soccer, and be a great teammate. If you're kind, helpful, and excited when you invite them, they'll feel more comfortable joining and will be excited to play.

In sales, it's the same idea. Selling isn't just about getting someone to buy your product. It's the first step in building a long-term relationship. If you sell in a way that's honest, supportive, and patient, your customer will trust you more. They'll be excited to work with you and will feel confident that they made the right choice.

How Sales Sets the Stage for a Strong Relationship

The way you sell to someone shows them what it will be like to work with you. If you're helpful, patient, and really listen to their needs, they'll think, "Wow, this person really cares about me." And when customers feel cared for, they're more likely to stick with your program, use your product, and get great results.

Example: Imagine you're selling piano lessons. Instead of just saying, "Sign up now!" you take the time to ask your customer, "What kind of music do you want to learn? What are your goals?" By showing them that you care about their interests, they'll trust you more and feel excited to start learning.

Building Trust from the First Conversation

When you're talking to a potential customer, think of it like planting a seed. The way you talk to them, answer their questions, and show your commitment is like watering that seed. If you do it right, it will grow into a strong, trusting relationship.

Here's how to build trust right from the start:

1. Listen Carefully to Their Needs

Imagine you're trying to convince a friend to come camping with you. If they say, "I'm not sure because I don't like bugs," you wouldn't just ignore that concern and say, "Come anyway!" Instead, you'd reassure them by saying, "I have bug spray and a comfy tent. You'll be safe and comfortable."

In sales, it's important to really listen to your customer's concerns and show them how your product can help solve their problems.

- **Tip**: Ask questions like, "What are you looking to achieve?" or "What's your biggest worry?" Then, show how your product or service can help.

2. Be Patient and Don't Rush the Sale

Imagine if you were trying to convince your friend to watch a movie they've never heard of. If you keep saying, "Come on, watch it right now!" they might feel pressured and say no. But if you say, "I think you'd really enjoy it, and we can watch it whenever you're ready," they'll feel more comfortable and might even get excited to watch it.

In sales, patience is key. When you give your customers the time and space to think about their decision, they'll feel less pressured and more confident in saying "yes."

Tip: Instead of pushing someone to buy right away, say, "Take your time to think about it. I'm here if you have any questions." This makes them feel supported rather than pressured.

Using Sales as the First Step in Coaching

Think of selling as the first coaching session with your customer. How you treat them during the sale is how they'll expect you to treat them once they've signed up. If you're supportive and helpful, they'll feel excited to work with you because they know you'll be there to guide them.

Example: Imagine you're selling a fitness coaching program. During your sales conversation, you take the time to understand their fitness goals, their struggles, and their concerns. When they see how much you care, they'll be more committed to working hard in your program because they trust that you're there to help them succeed.

The Benefits of Selling with a Coaching Mindset

When you sell with a coaching mindset, it shows your customer that you're not just trying to make money—you're genuinely interested in helping them succeed. This helps build a strong foundation of trust that makes your customer more likely to stick with your program, follow your advice, and see great results.

1. It Increases Customer Success

If your customers feel supported from the beginning, they'll be more motivated to use your product or follow your program. This means they're more likely to see results, which leads to happier customers and more referrals.

2. It Reduces Buyer's Remorse

Sometimes, after people buy something, they worry that they made the wrong choice. But if they feel supported and guided from the start, they'll feel good about their decision. This is called reducing "buyer's remorse."

Example: Let's say you sold a 6-month coaching program. After the customer signs up, you send them a welcome message saying, "I'm so excited to work with you! I'll be here every step of the way to help you reach your goals." This helps them feel confident that they made the right choice.

Key Takeaways

1. **Sales is the first step in coaching**: The way you sell sets the tone for your relationship with your customer.
2. **Listen, don't rush**: Show your customers that you care about their needs and give them time to make a decision.
3. **Build trust from the beginning**: When customers feel supported, they're more likely to succeed with your product or program.

Action Step: The next time you're talking to a potential customer, treat it like a coaching session. Ask questions, listen to their concerns, and show them how you can help. This will build trust and make them excited to work with you.

End of Chapter Challenge

Here's your challenge: Practise treating your next sales conversation as if you're already coaching the person. Instead of focusing on closing the sale, focus on understanding their needs and showing them how you can help. Notice how this changes the way they respond!

8

Putting the Client's Needs First – Selling with Curiosity and Care

Why You Should Focus on Helping, Not Just Selling

Imagine you're trying to help your friend decide which book to read next. If you only focus on getting them to pick your favourite book, they might not end up happy. But if you take the time to understand what they enjoy—like mysteries or adventure stories—you can recommend something they'll truly love.

In sales, it's the same. The most successful salespeople are the ones who truly care about their customers' needs. Instead of focusing on just closing the deal, they focus on helping the customer find what's best for them. This makes the customer feel valued, heard, and understood.

Example: Let's say you're selling a set of art supplies. Instead of just saying, "You should buy this," ask your customer, "What kind of art do you like to create?" By understanding their needs, you can show them how your product will help them make their best artwork.

The Secret to Building Strong Relationships: Childlike Curiosity

Have you ever seen a little kid ask a million questions? "Why is the sky blue?" "How do aeroplanes fly?" They're not trying to argue or prove a point—they're just curious. In sales, you can learn a lot from that kind of curiosity.

When you talk to a potential customer, practice asking questions with genuine curiosity. This shows that you care about their thoughts and feelings. Plus, it helps you understand what they really need.

Tip: If a customer hesitates or has doubts, don't try to convince them right away. Instead, say something like, "That's interesting! What makes you feel that way?" This helps the customer open up, and it can reveal the real reason they're hesitant.

How to Shift the Focus to the Customer's Needs

When you focus on truly understanding your customer, you can create a deeper connection. Here's how to do it:

1. Ask Open-Ended Questions

Instead of asking questions that can be answered with a simple "yes" or "no," ask questions that encourage your customer to share more.

- **Example**: If someone is unsure about buying your fitness program, instead of asking, "Do you want to sign up?" try asking, "What's your biggest fitness goal right now?" This helps you understand what they're looking for and how your program can help.

2. Show Empathy and Listen Carefully

Imagine your friend is nervous about trying out for the school play. Instead of saying, "You'll be fine, just do it," you can ask, "What's making you nervous?" By showing that you understand how they feel, you build trust.

In sales, listening is one of the most powerful tools you have. When a customer feels heard, they're more likely to trust you and buy from you.

Using Curiosity to Uncover Real Objections

Sometimes, customers will hesitate because they have concerns they haven't shared yet. Instead of pushing them to buy, use curiosity to understand what's holding them back.

Here's how to do it:

1. Respond with Curiosity, Not Arguments

If a customer says, "I'm not sure if I need this," don't argue or try to convince them right away. Instead, respond with, "That's interesting! What makes you feel unsure?" This opens up the conversation and helps you learn more about their concerns.

- **Example**: Let's say you're selling an online course, and your customer says, "I don't think I have time for this." You can respond with, "That's a fair point! What's taking up most of your time right now?" This way, you can find out if there's a way to fit your course into their schedule.

2. Keep Digging Deeper

Sometimes, the first concern a customer shares isn't the real issue. Use follow-up questions to dig deeper.

- **Example**: If a customer says, "I don't think I can afford it," ask, "What's your main concern about the cost?" You might discover that they're worried about making a big commitment upfront. Once you know that, you can offer a payment plan or smaller package.

How This Approach Builds Trust and Loyalty

When customers feel that you truly care about their needs, they're more likely to trust you. And when they trust you, they're not just buying a product—they're building a relationship with you. This leads to more sales, happier customers, and long-term loyalty.

Example: Imagine you're selling pet supplies. Instead of just saying, "Buy this new dog bed," you ask, "What does your dog love the most? A soft bed or a cosy blanket?" By showing that you care about their pet, you're more likely to earn their trust and their business.

The Benefits of a Client-Centred Approach

Here are a few reasons why focusing on your customer's needs is a game-changer in sales:

1. **Higher Satisfaction**: When customers feel heard and understood,

they're more satisfied with their purchase.

2. **More Referrals**: Happy customers are more likely to tell their friends about you.
3. **Stronger Relationships**: By focusing on what's best for the customer, you create long-term loyalty.

Key Takeaways

1. **Put your customer's needs first**: Focus on helping them, not just closing the sale.
2. **Be curious, not pushy**: Use questions to understand their concerns and needs.
3. **Listen carefully**: When customers feel heard, they trust you more.

Action Step: The next time you talk to a customer, practice asking questions with curiosity. Instead of trying to convince them to buy, focus on understanding what they truly need.

End of Chapter Challenge

Here's your challenge: Find a friend or family member and practice asking open-ended questions about something they're interested in. Instead of trying to prove your point, focus on understanding what they think and feel. See how much you can learn by just being curious!

9

Why Sales is About Empowering Clients, Not Pressuring Them

Imagine you're helping your friend decide which game to play next. You have your favourite game, and you really want them to play it with you. But instead of saying, "You have to play this game!" you say, "Here are the games we have. What do you think you'd enjoy the most?" By letting your friend choose, you're helping them feel more confident and happy with their decision.

In sales, it's the same. The goal isn't to pressure someone into buying something they're unsure about. Instead, it's about **empowering** them to make a decision that feels right for them. This way, they'll feel good about their choice and trust you more.

How Power in Sales Comes from Guiding, Not Pushing

Have you ever been at a store and felt like the salesperson was trying too hard to get you to buy something? It probably made you feel uncomfortable, right? But if a salesperson listens to you, helps you understand your options, and lets you decide, it feels much better.

The power in selling comes from being a guide, not a pusher. When you help customers see the benefits, understand their options, and make a choice for themselves, they feel more in control. This builds trust and makes them happier with their purchase.

Example: Imagine you're selling a science kit to a parent who wants their child to learn more about experiments. Instead of saying, "You need to buy this kit now!" you could say, "Here's how this kit can help your child learn and have fun. What do you think would work best for your child's learning style?" This helps the parent feel empowered to make the right choice.

Providing Clarity Leads to Confident Decisions

When customers are confused or unsure, they're less likely to buy. Your job as a salesperson is to provide clarity so that they feel confident in their decision.

Here's how to help your customers make clear, confident decisions:

1. Simplify Their Options

Too many choices can make people feel overwhelmed. Imagine you're at an ice cream shop with 50 flavours to choose from. It might take a long time to decide! But if there are only 3 flavours, it's much easier to pick.

Tip: If you're selling multiple products, help your customer narrow down their choices. Ask, "What are the most features you're looking for?" and guide them to the best option.

2. Use the "What's Best for You?" Approach

Instead of saying, "You should buy this," try asking, "What do you think would be best for you?" This puts the power back in their hands and makes them feel more confident about their decision.

- **Example**: Let's say you're selling a subscription service for learning new skills. Instead of pushing them to sign up, say, "Based on what you've told me, this service could help you reach your goals faster. But what do you think would work best for your schedule?"

This question shows that you're not just trying to sell something—you're trying to help them make the best choice for themselves.

Empowering Clients Builds Long-Term Trust

When clients feel empowered, they trust you more. They see you not as someone who's just trying to make a sale, but as a partner who truly cares about their needs.

Example: Imagine you're helping someone pick a gift for their child. Instead of pushing the most expensive option, you ask, "What does your child enjoy the most?" By helping them find the perfect gift based on their child's interests, they'll trust your advice more.

How to Empower Clients During the Sales Process

Here are some simple ways to empower your clients and build trust:

1. Ask Questions to Understand Their Needs

Before recommending anything, ask questions like, "What's most important to you?" or "What are you hoping to achieve?" This shows that you care about their goals, not just about making a sale.

Action Tip: The next time you're talking to a customer, spend the first few minutes just asking questions to understand what they need. This will help you recommend the best solution for them.

2. Encourage Them to Take Their Time

Sometimes, customers need time to think before making a decision. Instead of pushing them to buy right away, give them the space they need.

- **Example**: If someone says they're not sure, respond with, "That's completely fine! Take your time to think about it, and let me know if you have any questions. I'm here to help." This makes them feel supported and reduces the pressure to decide immediately.

3. Offer Honest Advice, Even if It Means Losing the Sale

Building trust means being honest, even if it's not in your best interest. If you know that your product might not be the best fit for a customer, tell them. They'll appreciate your honesty and are more likely to come back to you in the future.

Example: If a customer is looking for a specific feature that your product doesn't have, you can say, "I want to make sure you get what's best for you, and it looks like this might not be the perfect fit. Here's what I would recommend instead." This shows that you're truly looking out for them.

Key Takeaways

1. **Empower your clients**: Help them make decisions by guiding them, not pushing them.
2. **Provide clarity**: Make it easy for customers to understand their options and feel confident in their choice.
3. **Ask questions and listen**: Focus on understanding their needs so you can offer the best solution.

Action Step: The next time you're in a sales conversation, try using the "What's best for you?" approach. Focus on guiding your customer rather than pushing them to buy, and notice how they respond.

End of Chapter Challenge

Here's your challenge: Practise guiding a friend or family member through a decision. Ask questions to understand what they're looking for, offer options, and let them choose what feels best for them. Notice how this changes the conversation and builds trust!

10

Mastering Objections – Turning "No" into "Yes"

What are Objections?

I magine you're trying to convince your friend to come over and play video games at your house. But your friend says:

- "I can't, I have homework."
- "I don't know if I'm allowed."
- "I'm tired, maybe another time."

These are called **objections**. It's when someone says, "I can't" or "I don't want to" because they have reasons (or excuses) for not doing what you're asking them to do.In sales, objections happen a lot. People don't always say "yes" right away, even if they want what you're offering. But here's the secret: when someone says "no," it doesn't always mean they really don't want it. It usually means they just have some worries or questions that you need to help them with.

The Difference Between Obstacles and Objections

Let's break it down using a simple example:

Imagine you have a cookie stand, and you're trying to sell cookies to your neighbours.

- **Obstacle**: Your neighbour says, "I'm just looking; I don't want any cookies right now." (This means they're not ready to buy yet.)
- **Objection**: Your neighbour says, "I would buy a cookie, but I don't have any money on me." (This is something specific stopping them from buying.)

Obstacles are things that people say before they are even ready to decide. **Objections** are reasons they have once they're thinking about buying but need a little more convincing.

The Top Objections in Sales

Let's look at some common objections that people might have when you're trying to sell something, and how you can handle them using

1. **Objection**: "I don't have enough time"

- **Example**: Imagine you're selling a new online course that teaches kids how to draw cool cartoons.
- **Customer**: "I don't have time to take this course."

2.**Objection**: "It's too expensive"

- **Example**: Imagine you're selling a fancy new bike to your neighbour.
- **Customer**: "That bike is too expensive. I can't afford it."

3 .**Objection**: "I need to think about it"

- **Example**: Imagine you're trying to sell a board game to your friend.
- **Customer**: "I need to think about it. I'm not sure."

1. **Objection**: "I need to consult with my partner"

- **Example**: Imagine you're selling a personal training program.
- **Customer**: "I need to talk to my partner before making a decision."

1. **Objection**: "I don't think it will work for me"

- **Example**: Imagine you're selling a weight loss coaching program.
- **Customer**: "I've tried things like this before, and they didn't work."

6. **Objection**: "I don't have the money right now"

- **Example**: Imagine you're selling a financial coaching course.
- **Customer**: "I can't afford this program right now."

7. **Objection**: "It's not the right time for me"

- **Example**: Imagine you're selling a fitness membership.
- **Customer**: "I'm really busy right now. Maybe later."

8. **Objection**: "I'm not sure if it fits my needs"

- **Example**: Imagine you're selling a dietary supplement.
- **Customer**: "I'm not sure if this is right for me."

9. **Objection**: "I've been burned before"

- **Example**: Imagine you're selling a digital marketing service.
- **Customer**: "I've tried something like this before, and it didn't work."

11

Overcoming the Biggest Objection - "It's Too Expensive"

Why People Say "It's Too Expensive"

Imagine you're trying to convince your parents to buy you a very fancy new gaming console that costs a lot of money. It's not that they don't want you to have it; they just need to be convinced that it's worth spending so much money.

In sales, people often say, "It's too expensive" not because they don't want what you're offering, but because they're not sure if it's really worth the high price. Your job is to help them see why the product is worth the money.

Turning "Too Expensive" into "Worth Every Penny"

Let's say you're selling something big—like a luxury vacation package, an expensive online coaching program, or a high-end piece of technology. These items can cost thousands of dollars, so it's natural for people to hesitate and say, "That's too expensive!"

But as Alex Hormozi teaches, you can still turn that "no" into a "yes" by helping people see the value.

Example 1: Selling a Luxury Vacation Package

Imagine you're selling a vacation package to a beautiful tropical island. The package includes five-star hotel accommodations, guided tours, and gourmet meals. But it costs $5,000, and your customer says, "I can't spend that much on a vacation."

Here's how you can handle it:

- **You**: "I totally understand, it's a big investment. But think about it— this is a once-in-a-lifetime experience. Imagine waking up to a view of the ocean, enjoying meals prepared by world-class chefs, and making memories that will last forever. If you consider the quality of the experience and the memories you'll create, it's really worth it. Plus, everything is taken care of for you, so you don't have to worry about anything."

Tip: When selling high-ticket products like luxury vacations, focus on the **experience** and the **lifetime memories** that come with it.

Example 2: Selling a $10,000 Online Coaching Program

Let's say you're selling a high-ticket online coaching program that helps people start their own business. It costs $10,000, and your potential customer says, "That's way too expensive."

Here's how to respond:

- **You**: "I totally get it; $10,000 is a significant amount of money. But think of it this way: If this program helps you build a successful business that earns you $100,000 or more a year, wouldn't it be worth it? Plus, with the coaching, you're not just paying for information—you're paying for guidance, support, and a proven system that can save you years of trial and error. This investment can pay for itself many times over."

Tip: When selling high-ticket coaching programs, emphasise the **return on investment** (ROI) and how it can change their life in the long run.

Example 3: Selling a $3,000 High-End Laptop

Imagine you're selling a high-end laptop that costs $3,000. Your customer says, "Why would I spend that much on a laptop when I can get one for $500?"
Here's how you can handle that objection:

- **You**: "I totally understand. But let's think about what you're getting with this laptop. It has a super-fast processor, top-notch graphics, and a battery that lasts all day. If you're using it for work or creative projects, this laptop can help you be much more productive. Plus, it's built to last for years, so you won't have to replace it as often as a cheaper model. Over time, it can actually save you money."

Tip: For high-end technology, focus on **durability**, **performance**, and **long-term value**.

Three Ways to Handle "It's Too Expensive"

1. Compare It to Something They Already Buy

When selling high-ticket items, sometimes people don't realise they're already spending money on similar things. Let's say you're selling a $2,000 mattress that improves sleep quality.

- **Customer**: "That's way too much for a mattress!"
- **You**: "I totally understand. But think about it—how much do you spend on your health and well-being? If this mattress helps you sleep better, you'll have more energy, be more productive, and even improve your health. Isn't it worth investing in something that helps you feel great every day?"

Tip: Show them how your product is a smart investment for their health and well-being.

2. Break It Down into Smaller Parts

If someone is struggling with the high price of an executive coaching program that costs $12,000, break it down for them.

- **You**: "I know $12,000 seems like a lot, but let's break it down. That's only $1,000 a month, or about $33 a day. For the price of a coffee and a lunch, you're investing in a program that can transform your business and help you make tens of thousands more."

- **Tip**: Breaking down the cost helps people see how it fits into their budget more easily.**3. Focus on the Long-Term Value and Results**

Imagine you're selling a $5,000 high-ticket fitness program. Your customer says, "I can't spend that much on a fitness program."

- **You**: "I understand—it's a big decision. But let's think about what you're really investing in. This isn't just about losing a few pounds; it's about changing your entire lifestyle. With this program, you'll feel healthier, have more energy, and live longer. What's that worth to you? If it helps you avoid costly medical bills in the future, wouldn't that alone make it worth it?"

Tip: For high-ticket products, always emphasise the **long-term benefits** and how it can save money in other areas of life.

How to Know if "Too Expensive" is Really the Problem

Sometimes, when people say "it's too expensive," it's not really about the money. Here's a quick tip to find out if that's the case:

- **You**: "If money wasn't an issue, would you be ready to sign up today?"
- **Customer**: "Well, maybe... I'm not sure if this program will really work

for me."

- **You**: "Ah, so it's more about making sure it's the right fit for you. Let's talk about how this program has helped others just like you."

By asking this question, you can uncover if there's another reason behind their hesitation and address it.

Key Takeaways

1. **People want to buy, but they need to see the value**: For high-ticket products, show them why it's worth the price.
2. **Break down the cost**: Make it easier for people to see how they're getting great value for their money.
3. **Focus on the benefits and long-term results**: Help them see how your product will improve their life or business in the long run.

Action Step: Practise handling objections for high-ticket products by focusing on value, breaking down the cost, and comparing it to things people already spend money on.

12

Handling "I Need to Think About It" – Helping People Make Decisions

Why People Say, "I Need to Think About It"
Imagine you're trying to convince your friend to come over for a sleepover. You ask them, "Do you want to come over tonight?" And they say, "I need to think about it."

What they're really saying is that they're unsure. Maybe they're worried they won't have fun, or they're not sure if their parents will let them go. In sales, when people say, "I need to think about it," it usually means they have some doubts or worries that they haven't shared yet.

Helping People Feel Confident About Their Decision

Alex Hormozi teaches that when someone says, "I need to think about it," it doesn't mean they don't want what you're offering. It just means they're not sure if they're ready to make the commitment. Your job is to help them feel confident in making that decision right now.

Example: Think about when you're standing in front of an ice cream shop, trying to decide which flavour to get. You might hesitate because you don't want to pick the wrong one. But if a friend says, "Go with chocolate! You always love chocolate," it helps you make a decision quickly.

In sales, you can do the same thing—help your customer feel confident that they're making the right choice.

Three Reasons Why People Say "I Need to Think About It"

1. They're Afraid of Making a Mistake

Sometimes, people worry that if they make a decision too quickly, they might regret it later. Imagine your friend is trying to decide whether to buy a new skateboard. They might say, "I need to think about it," because they're afraid they'll find a better one somewhere else.

How to Handle It:

- **You**: "I totally understand. It's a big decision. But think about how much fun you'll have riding this skateboard today! Plus, if you don't get it now, it might sell out, and you might miss out on the fun."

Tip: Remind them of the good things they'll gain if they make the decision now.

2. They Don't Feel Confident Yet

Imagine you're trying to sell a cooking class to someone who doesn't know how to cook. They might say, "I need to think about it," because they're not sure if they can do it. They don't feel confident in their ability to succeed.

How to Handle It:

- **You**: "I get it. Learning something new can be a little scary. But that's why this class is perfect for beginners. We'll go step-by-step, and I'll be there to help you the whole way. You'll be making delicious meals in no time!"

Tip: Assure them that they're not alone and that your product or service is designed to help them succeed.

3. They Don't See How It Will Benefit Them Right Away

Sometimes, people can't see how your product or service will make a difference in their life right now. Imagine you're selling a yearly gym membership. The customer might say, "I need to think about it," because they're not sure if they'll actually use it.

How to Handle It:

- **You**: "I totally understand. But imagine how great you'll feel after just a few weeks of working out. You'll have more energy, feel healthier, and maybe even fit into your favourite jeans again. And if you start now, you'll already be ahead of your fitness goals for the year."
- **Tip**: Paint a picture of the benefits they'll experience if they take action now.

How to Turn "I Need to Think About It" into a "Yes"

Here are some easy ways to help someone make a decision when they say, "I need to think about it."

1. Use the "What's Holding You Back?" Question

If someone says they need to think about it, sometimes it's because they have a specific worry they haven't told you about. Try asking:

- **You**: "I understand you want to think about it. But can I ask, what's the biggest thing holding you back right now?"

This question helps them open up about their real concern. Once you know what's bothering them, you can address it directly.

2. Use the "Imagine If" Technique

Help them imagine the positive outcome of making the decision today. This is like saying, "Imagine if you had superpowers—wouldn't that be amazing?"

Example:

- **Customer**: "I need to think about it."
- **You**: "I get it. But imagine if you signed up today. By next month, you could already be seeing results. How great would it feel to be ahead of your goals instead of waiting and wondering?"

This technique helps them see the benefits of taking action now instead of delaying.

3. Offer a "No-Risk" Guarantee

Sometimes people are just afraid of making the wrong choice. Offering a no-risk guarantee can help them feel safe.

Example: Imagine you're selling a high-ticket online course that costs $1,000. The customer says, "I need to think about it."

- **You**: "I totally understand. That's why we offer a 30-day money-back guarantee. You can try the course, and if you're not happy, we'll refund you, no questions asked. That way, there's no risk. Would you like to give it a try?"

This helps them feel confident that they have nothing to lose.

Helping People Feel Comfortable Saying "Yes"

Remember, people don't want to feel pressured. They just want to make sure they're making the right choice. When you help them see the benefits, answer their questions, and reduce their fears, they'll feel more comfortable saying "yes."

Key Takeaways

1. **Listen to Understand**: When someone says "I need to think about it," it usually means they have a hidden worry. Your job is to find out what it is.
2. **Help Them Feel Confident**: Show them that they're making a smart decision.
3. **Reduce the Risk**: Offer guarantees or support to make them feel safe in saying "yes."

Action Step: Practise using the "What's Holding You Back?" and "Imagine If" techniques with your friends or family. The more you practise, the better you'll get at turning a "maybe" into a "yes!"

13

Overcoming Time-Related Objections

Understanding the "I Don't Have Time" Objection

I magine trying to get your friend to join you in a new hobby, like learning to play the guitar. They might say, "I don't have time right now." But often, the real reason isn't about time—it's about priorities, hesitation, or uncertainty about whether the effort will be worth it.

In sales, the **"I don't have time"** objection is common, but it often masks deeper concerns. Here's how to address these objections effectively using three powerful frameworks.

1. The Busy Season Argument

Sometimes clients say they're too busy because they're going through a hectic period at work, school, or home. However, if they're always waiting for a "better time," they may never get started.

How to Handle This Objection

- **Acknowledge Their Situation**: "I understand that you're super busy right now."
- **Ask About Future Busy Periods**: "Do you think you'll be less busy a few months from now? Or will there always be something that comes up?"
- **Reframe Busyness as an Advantage**: "If you start now while things are hectic, you'll be better prepared to handle busy times in the future. It's like training under real conditions—you'll develop the skills to manage everything more effectively."

Example: Imagine you're selling a time management course.

- **Customer**: "I'm too busy to take this course right now."
- **You**: "I totally get that. But if you're busy now, don't you think it would be even more helpful to learn strategies to manage your time better? That way, you can handle business more effectively whenever it comes up."

Tip: Help clients see that starting during a busy period can actually be an advantage, as it forces them to practise what they're learning in real-time.

2. Micro-Time Analysis

Often, people think they're too busy because they haven't taken a closer look at how they spend their day. In reality, they may be spending hours on activities that aren't aligned with their goals. By helping clients identify where their time is going, you can show them how they can fit your solution into their schedule.

How to Address Micro-Time Issues

- **Ask About Daily Routines**: "Can we take a quick look at your schedule? I've found that most people have small pockets of time they're not using efficiently."
- **Point Out Time-Wasters**: "I once had a client who thought she had no time, but when we looked at her schedule, we realised she was spending two hours a day on social media. By cutting that in half, she found time to pursue her goals."
- **Emphasise Efficiency**: "Our program is designed to streamline your schedule so you can free up time by eliminating non-essential activities."

Example: Imagine you're selling a fitness program.

- **Customer**: "I just don't have time to work out."
- **You**: "I totally get it. But let's think about it—how much time do you spend on social media or watching TV each day? If you just dedicated 20 minutes to a quick workout instead, you'd feel so much better."

Tip: Use examples to show how small adjustments can lead to big changes in their schedule and productivity.

3. The "When-Then" Fallacy

Many clients fall into the trap of thinking, "When I have more time, then I'll start." This mindset can keep them stuck because the perfect time rarely arrives. Instead, taking action now, even in small ways, leads to progress.

How to Overcome the "When-Then" Fallacy

- **Acknowledge Their Hesitation**: "I understand that you're waiting for the perfect time."
- **Explain the Fallacy**: "The truth is, waiting for the perfect moment often means never getting started. It's like waiting to save money until you're rich—it just doesn't work that way."
- **Encourage Taking a Small Step Now**: "What if you just dedicated 10 minutes a day to this? You'll be surprised at how much progress you can make without waiting for everything to be perfect."

Example: Imagine you're selling an online course.

- **Customer**: "I'll join when things calm down."
- **You**: "I get it, but the perfect time rarely comes. What if you just committed to watching one lesson a week? That small step will keep you moving forward, even if things are busy."

Tip: Reinforce that progress doesn't require a huge time commitment. Consistent small steps can lead to significant results over time.

Summary of Key Techniques

1. **Busy Season Argument**: Help clients see that starting now, even during busy times, prepares them to handle future challenges better.
2. **Micro-Time Analysis**: Address time objections by highlighting time-wasting activities and showing how your product can streamline their schedule.
3. **The "When-Then" Fallacy**: Encourage clients to take small, actionable steps now instead of waiting for the perfect time.

Key Takeaways

- The "I don't have time" objection is often about priorities, not actual time constraints.
- Reframe the conversation to show clients that starting now, even in small ways, is better than waiting.
- Help clients see the hidden pockets of time in their day that they can use more effectively.

End of Chapter Challenge

Here's your challenge: On your next sales call, when a client says they're too busy, use one of the frameworks from this chapter to address their concern. Notice how it changes their perspective and helps them see the value of taking action now.

14

Reframing Product Fit Concerns – Helping Clients See the Value

Why Clients Question Product Fit

I magine you're trying to convince your friend to join your basketball team, but they say, "I'm not sure if I'm good enough." What they really mean is that they're worried about not fitting in or not being able to keep up. In sales, when a client questions if your product is a good fit for them, it's usually because they're uncertain about their ability to succeed or they're afraid of change.The good news? You can help clients overcome this doubt by reframing how they see themselves and by addressing their concerns in a positive way.

Three Strategies to Handle Fit Objections

When clients say, "I'm not sure if this is right for me," it's your job to understand where that hesitation is coming from. Here are three approaches to help them overcome these doubts.

Strategy 1: Aligning New Identity with New Priorities Sometimes, clients resist buying because they haven't fully embraced the idea of becoming the kind of person who invests in themselves. It's like when kids start using their allowance to buy grown-up things, like makeup or cool gadgets—they're stepping into a new identity.

How to Handle It:

- **You**: "I understand that investing in this might feel new. It's kind of like when someone first starts budgeting for healthier food or exercise equipment. It's about stepping into a new version of yourself. Just like young girls start buying makeup to feel more grown-up, investing in this program is about aligning your actions with the future you want."

Example: Imagine you're selling a self-improvement course, and the client says, "I don't usually spend money on things like this." You can say, "That's completely normal when you're shifting priorities. Think of it like taking your first step into a new chapter. By investing in yourself, you're showing that you're ready to grow and achieve new goals." **Strategy 2: Changing Habits for New Outcomes** Clients sometimes hesitate because your product requires them to change their habits. They might say, "I don't think I can stick to that diet plan" or "I don't have time for those exercises." The truth is, their current routines are part of what got them to where they are now, and if they want different results, they need to change something.

How to Handle It:

- **You**: "I totally get that it's hard to change routines. But here's the thing—our current habits have brought us to where we are today. If we want different results, we have to try something new. For example, the breakfast you're used to eating might be why you're feeling low on energy. Let's try something different to help you feel better."

Example: If someone says they can't find time for your coaching program, say, "I understand—it's tough to change routines. But imagine if just a small shift in your daily habits could lead to big changes. If you spend even 10 minutes a day on this, it could transform your results."

Strategy 12 : Hypothetical Testing of Objections

Sometimes, clients aren't sure if your program is the right fit because they're afraid of failing. To get to the bottom of this, use a technique called **hypothetical testing**. This helps you figure out if their hesitation is about the program itself or if it's something deeper.

How to Handle It:

- **You**: "Let's imagine for a moment that this program is perfect for you and fits all your needs exactly. Would you still hesitate to join?"

If the client says "yes," it means there's a deeper fear, like a fear of failure or self-doubt. If they say "no," then their hesitation is about a specific part of the program, which you can address directly. **Example**: Let's say someone hesitates to buy your fitness program because they're not sure if they can stick with it. You can ask, "If this program fit perfectly into your schedule and you knew you'd get great results, would you still hesitate?" If they say yes, you can explore their fear of failure. If they say no, you can adjust the program to better fit their schedule.

Practical Examples for Each Strategy

1. **Aligning New Identity**:

- **Client**: "I don't usually spend money on coaching programs."
- **You**: "I totally understand. But investing in yourself is like stepping into a new role, just like when someone buys their first suit for a job interview. It's about showing that you're ready to grow."

1. **Changing Habits**:

- **Client**: "I don't think I can commit to that meal plan."
- **You**: "I get it—changing what we're used to is tough. But if we want new results, we have to try something different. Let's start small and adjust it to fit your tastes."

1. **Hypothetical Testing**:

- **Client**: "I'm not sure if this is the right program for me."
- **You**: "Let's say this program fit all your needs perfectly—would you still hesitate? If so, let's talk about what's really holding you back."

Why These Approaches Work

By aligning your client's new goals with their identity, helping them change habits, and addressing deeper fears, you can turn their hesitation into confidence. These techniques show that you're not just trying to sell them something—you're genuinely interested in helping them succeed.

Key Takeaways

1. **Align new priorities with identity**: Help clients see how investing in themselves is part of their growth journey.
2. **Encourage small habit changes**: Show that changing routines can lead to new, better results.
3. **Use hypothetical testing**: Uncover whether the client's hesitation is about the program or a deeper fear.

Action Step: Practise using one of these strategies with a friend or client who's unsure about committing. See if you can help them feel more confident about their decision.

End of Chapter Challenge

Here's your challenge: The next time someone hesitates because they're unsure if your product is a good fit, try using one of these strategies. Focus on understanding their concerns and reframing them in a positive way. Notice how this changes their response!

15

Handling Authority Objections – Empowering Clients to Take Ownership

Why People Say They Need Permission Imagine you're trying to convince your friend to come to a sleepover, but they say, "I have to check with my parents first." In reality, they might be unsure of themselves and using their parents as a reason to delay saying yes or no. In sales, clients often do the same thing. When someone says, "I need to talk to my partner" or "I need approval from my boss," it's often because they're not fully confident in their own decision. But here's the good news: you can help them take ownership of their decision and feel more confident. Let's explore how to do that!

Three Strategies to Handle Authority Objections

When clients say they need permission, it's your job to dig a little deeper and help them feel empowered. Here are three strategies to handle these objections effectively.

1: Encouraging Ownership and Support

Sometimes, clients say they need to ask for permission because they're afraid of making a decision on their own. One way to overcome this is to shift their mindset from seeking "permission" to seeking "support." This helps them feel more empowered to take action.

How to Handle It:

- **You**: "I completely understand that you want to check with your partner. But let me ask—do you think they would support you in achieving your goals? It's not about getting permission, but about helping them understand how this can benefit you."

Example: If a client is hesitant to sign up for a fitness program because they want to check with their partner, you could say, "I'm sure your partner wants you to feel healthier and happier. Let's focus on how you can share this exciting journey with them, rather than asking for permission."

Tip: Reframing it as seeking support rather than approval helps clients feel like they're making a joint decision, not just waiting for someone else's say-so.

Strategy 2: Isolating Objections

When clients say they need to check with someone else, it's often a way of hiding their own doubts. By gently digging deeper, you can find out if the objection is truly about someone else—or if it's the client's own concerns.

How to Handle It:

- **You**: "I understand you want to talk to your partner about this. Can I ask—what do you think they wouldn't like about this decision?"

This question helps reveal if the concern is really about the partner or if it's actually the client's hesitation. If they can't think of anything specific, it usually means the objection is coming from within. **Example**: If someone says, "I need to talk to my boss before buying this training program," you could ask, "What do you think your boss would be concerned about?" If they struggle to answer, you've uncovered that the hesitation is likely their own. **Tip**: Once you identify the real concern, address it directly. This can help the client feel more confident in making their own decision.

Strategy 3: Framing the Consequences of Deferral

Sometimes, clients defer decisions because they're afraid of taking full responsibility. However, if they constantly put off making decisions for themselves, they might end up feeling resentful toward the people they rely on for "permission." Your job is to show them that taking ownership now can actually improve their relationships and lead to greater personal success.

How to Handle It:

- **You**: "I understand you want to consult your partner. But here's something to think about—if you keep waiting for permission, you might later feel frustrated that you never took action when you had the chance. This is your goal, and achieving it is something that can improve your life.

How would it feel to have their support instead of needing their permission?" **Example**: Imagine a client says, "I need to check with my spouse before I sign up for this course." You can respond, "I understand, but consider this—if you keep waiting for the perfect moment, you might never take the steps to reach your goals. Wouldn't it feel great to tell your partner that you're taking this step to better yourself?" **Tip**: Framing the decision as a way to seek support for personal growth rather than deferring to someone else can empower clients to take charge of their own success.

Practical Examples for Each Strategy

1. **Encouraging Ownership**:

- **Client**: "I need to ask my partner first."
- **You**: "I totally understand. But I'm sure your partner wants the best for you. Let's talk about how this program can bring positive changes to your life that they'd be excited to support."

1. **Isolating Objections**:

- **Client**: "I need to talk to my boss."
- **You**: "What do you think they might not like about this? Let's see if we can address any concerns together."

1. **Framing the Consequences**:

SALES MASTERY

- **Client**: "I need to wait until my partner agrees."
- **You**: "I understand. But remember, this is about your goals and dreams. Sometimes, taking action for yourself can inspire others to support you even more."

Why These Approaches Work

By shifting the conversation from "permission" to "support," isolating hidden objections, and reframing the consequences of deferral, you empower clients to take ownership of their decisions. This helps build trust, increases confidence, and shows that you genuinely care about their success.

Key Takeaways

1. **Encourage clients to seek support, not permission**: Help them feel empowered in their decisions.
2. **Dig deeper to uncover hidden concerns**: Address the client's real doubts, not just the surface objections.
3. **Reframe deferral as a potential regret**: Show clients the benefits of taking charge of their decisions now.

Action Step: The next time a client says they need to consult someone, try using one of these strategies. Focus on helping them feel confident in making the decision for themselves.

End of Chapter Challenge

Here's your challenge: Practise handling authority objections with a friend or colleague. Role-play a scenario where they say, "I need to ask for permission." Use the techniques in this chapter to guide them toward taking ownership of the decision. Notice how this changes their response!

16

Managing Avoidance and Decision Paralysis

Why Clients Get Stuck in Decision Paralysis

Imagine you're trying to convince your friend to join a new club at school, and they keep saying, "I'm interested, but I need to think about it." Weeks go by, and they still haven't made a decision. The real problem isn't that they need more time—it's that they're afraid of making the wrong choice.

In sales, clients often get stuck in **decision paralysis** because they're afraid of making a mistake. They might seem interested, but they keep delaying because of hidden fears or doubts. Your job is to help them move past this hesitation so they can make a decision that benefits them.

Three Strategies to Overcome Decision Paralysis

When clients keep delaying, it's a sign that they're unsure. Here's how to help them get unstuck and take action.

Strategy 1: Addressing Past Hesitation Patterns

If clients have a history of hesitating on important decisions, it's helpful to gently point out this pattern. Sometimes, they need a reminder that their current hesitation is part of an old habit that's been holding them back.

How to Handle It:

- **You**: "I get that you're feeling unsure. But let's think about it—do you think part of why you're still in this situation is because you've hesitated on similar decisions in the past? This could be your chance to break that cycle and finally move forward."

Example: If a client keeps delaying a decision to join a business coaching program, you could say, "It seems like you've been wanting to grow your business for a while, but something keeps holding you back. What if this hesitation is the exact thing that's been stopping you from reaching your goals?"

Tip: By acknowledging their hesitation pattern, you help clients see that taking action now is an opportunity to break free from their past indecision.

Strategy 2: Focusing on Present Reality and Information Needs

Sometimes, clients think they need more time to decide when what they actually need is more information. Help them understand that time alone won't make the decision easier—what they need is clarity.

How to Handle It:

- **You**: "I understand that you feel like you need more time. But often, effective decisions are made based on information, not just time. Let's go over any questions you have right now so you can make the best decision without delaying further."

Example: If a client says they're not ready to commit to a fitness program, you can say, "I know it feels like you need more time to think about it, but what questions or concerns do you have that I can answer now? The more information you have, the easier it will be to decide."

Tip: By focusing on providing information, you can help clients feel more confident and ready to take action without delay.

Strategy 3: Highlighting the Future Cost of Inaction

Often, clients don't realise the long-term cost of delaying a decision. Use visualisation to help them see the impact of staying in the same place for years to come.

How to Handle It:

- **You**: "Let's imagine it's five years from now, and you're still facing the same challenges you are today. How would that feel? Would you be happy with where you're at? Sometimes, the cost of not acting now is much greater than the cost of making a decision today."

Example: If someone is hesitant to join your personal development course, say, "Imagine yourself five years from now, still feeling stuck in the same patterns. Would you wish you had taken action sooner? This could be your chance to change that story."

Tip: By focusing on the future, you can help clients realise that the best time to act is now, not later.

Practical Examples for Each Strategy

1. **Addressing Past Hesitation Patterns**:

- **Client**: "I've been thinking about this for a while, but I'm still unsure."
- **You**: "I understand. But do you think part of why you're still in this position is because you've hesitated on decisions like this before? What if taking action now is the breakthrough you've been waiting for?"

1. **Focusing on Present Reality**:

- **Client**: "I just need more time to think it over."
- **You**: "I get it. But let's make sure you have all the information you need now so you can make a confident decision without waiting longer than necessary."

1. **Highlighting the Future Cost of Inaction**:

- **Client**: "I'm not sure if I'm ready to commit."
- **You**: "Let's imagine how things might look five years from now if nothing changes. Would you feel satisfied if you were still facing the same struggles?"

These Approaches Work

These strategies help clients move past their hesitation by addressing the root causes of their indecision. Whether it's a pattern of past hesitation, a lack of clarity, or fear of future regret, you're helping them see the benefits of making a decision now.

Key Takeaways

1. **Break the hesitation pattern**: Help clients recognize when they're falling into old habits of indecision.
2. **Provide clarity, not just time**: Focus on answering questions and providing information so clients feel ready to decide.
3. **Highlight the future cost of inaction**: Use visualisation to show that delaying decisions often leads to regret and missed opportunities.

Action Step: The next time a client keeps delaying, try using one of these strategies. Focus on helping them overcome their hesitation by addressing the real concerns behind their indecision.

End of Chapter Challenge

Here's your challenge: Find a friend or colleague who's been hesitating on a decision. Practice using the strategies in this chapter to help them see the benefits of taking action now. See if you can help them move forward with confidence!

17

Advanced Objection Handling and Closing Techniques

After working through objections, you may still encounter hesitation. This part focuses on guiding clients past avoidance and helping them feel confident in their choice. The strategies here aim to address any remaining doubts and empower clients to make a commitment.

1. Navigating Final Objections and Avoidance

When clients have exhausted their initial objections, they often default to vague avoidance statements like, "I need to think about it." This is usually the last defence, indicating that all practical concerns are addressed, but emotional hesitation remains. Here's how to overcome this avoidance step-by-step:

- **Past Hesitation Pattern**: If clients have historically delayed decisions, ask, "Have you ever hesitated like this on a similar decision? Do you think that might be why you're still in this position?" By highlighting this pattern, you create an opportunity for them to break the cycle of indecision.

- **The "Rocking Chair" Approach for Present Avoidance**: Help clients realise that they don't need additional time; they need more clarity. Describe a relatable scenario, like sitting in a rocking chair thinking about the decision. Remind them that time won't provide new information— only action will bring change. By emphasising that you're available to answer any questions now, you guide them toward making a choice without delaying.

- **Future Avoidance and Inaction Costs**: Project the potential cost of inaction. Ask the client to envision themselves in five years, still dealing with the same issues because they delayed. This approach magnifies the negative impact of postponing a decision, helping them understand that inaction may cost them far more than committing to the solution today.

2. Using the "Three-Question" Decision Framework

When clients need a structured decision-making approach, the "Three-Question" framework is highly effective. It encourages them to focus on key factors and arrive at a choice they feel good about:

- **Question 1: "Does This Product Help You Achieve Your Goals?"** Start by asking if they believe the product or service will move them closer to their goals. This shifts their focus to their goals and whether the product aligns with their vision for success.

- **Question 2: "Do You Trust Me to Deliver on My Promises?"** Trust is essential for a successful sale. Confirm whether they feel confident in your ability to provide what you've promised. If they hesitate, explore their concerns to build rapport and reassurance.

- **Question 3: "Do You Think It Will Work Specifically for You?"** This final question addresses personal doubts. If they're unsure, ask, "Why not?" which gives them a chance to voice lingering concerns. This process encourages clients to reflect on their own belief in their potential, often leading to a positive commitment.

When clients answer "yes" to all three questions, they'll feel more certain in their decision to move forward.

3. Closing Techniques for Commitment with Minimal Pressure

These closing techniques help clients make a final decision without feeling pressured, enhancing their comfort and satisfaction with the choice:

- **The Guarantee-Based Close**: If your product includes a trial or guarantee, use this to alleviate concerns. Emphasise that clients are simply making an "informed decision," which only becomes final after they've had a chance to experience the product. This low-pressure close builds confidence and reduces risk, encouraging clients to try it with the assurance of a fallback.

- **"Which Future Are We Killing Today?" Technique**: Explain the origin of the word "decide" (from the Latin "decidere," meaning "to cut off"). Tell the client that every decision "kills" a potential future: one where they continue as is, or one where they choose change. This reframes the choice as empowering—deciding to "kill" the past in favour of a better future.

- **Future-Paced Frame**: Ask them to consider, "What will my life look like if I stay where I am versus if I make this change?" This thought exercise highlights the benefits of moving forward and gives a tangible perspective on the consequences of delay versus action.

4. Framing the Product as Directional Progress Rather Than Perfection

Clients often hesitate due to a fear that the product or service won't be the perfect solution. Remind them that achieving goals doesn't require perfection but rather a steady move in the right direction.

- **Directional Progress Over Perfection**: Ask if this decision will bring them "closer to or further from" their goal. Explain that they don't need to find the perfect solution; they simply need to make choices that align with their goals. Over time, consistent steps forward compound to produce transformative results. This alleviates perfectionistic concerns and encourages clients to take the first step.

- **Accumulated Value of Education and Improvement**: Share that while no single program will likely transform everything, each investment builds on the last. For instance, learning, training, or coaching is a continual journey that adds layers of improvement. This cumulative approach allows clients to see the decision as a valuable contribution to their long-term success rather than a one-time solution.

5. "The Reason You Should Do This Is the Reason You're Hesitating" Close

This closing technique addresses the core hesitation often buried beneath layers of objections. It's particularly effective with clients who voice a specific reason for holding back.

- **Reframing Hesitation as Motivation**: If a client says they "can't afford it," suggest that this financial hesitation is the exact reason they should take action. Explain that the financial commitment will push them to engage fully and improve their financial situation. Or if they're concerned about lack of time, mention that committing will help them reclaim time by focusing on the essentials.

- **Example Response**: "If you're hesitating because of the cost, it's because you're not where you want to be financially. This program can help you change that by teaching you skills that directly impact your income." This approach reframes their biggest concern as their most compelling reason to proceed.

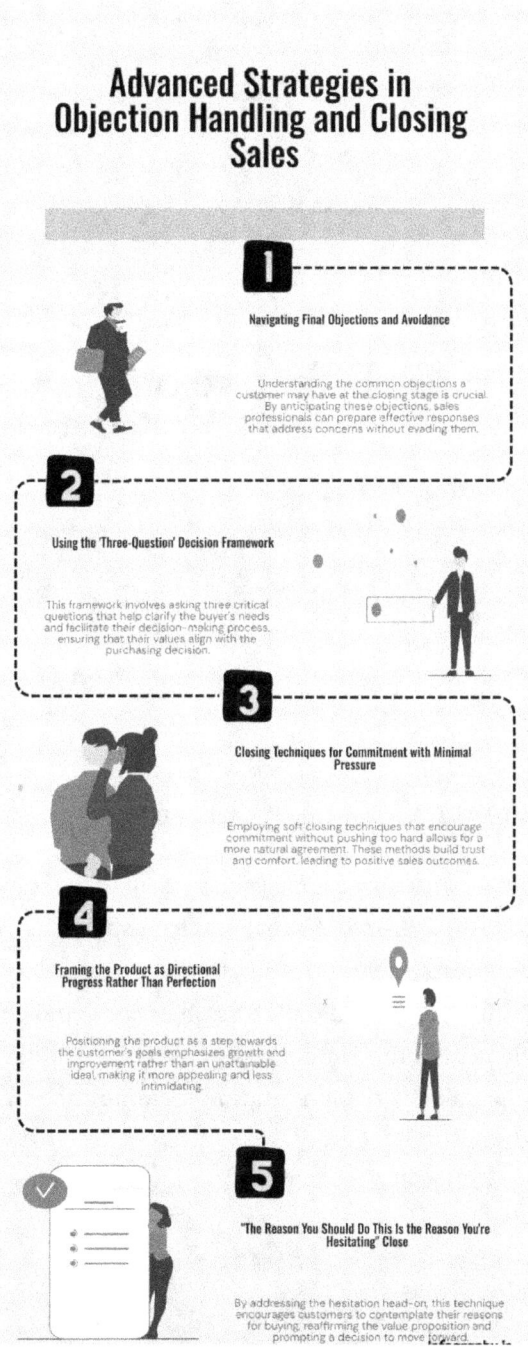

Advanced Strategies in Objection Handling and Closing Sales

1

Navigating Final Objections and Avoidance

Understanding the common objections a customer may have at the closing stage is crucial. By anticipating these objections, sales professionals can prepare effective responses that address concerns without evading them.

2

Using the 'Three-Question' Decision Framework

This framework involves asking three critical questions that help clarify the buyer's needs and facilitate their decision-making process, ensuring that their values align with the purchasing decision.

3

Closing Techniques for Commitment with Minimal Pressure

Employing soft closing techniques that encourage commitment without pushing too hard allows for a more natural agreement. These methods build trust and comfort, leading to positive sales outcomes.

4

Framing the Product as Directional Progress Rather Than Perfection

Positioning the product as a step towards the customer's goals emphasizes growth and improvement rather than an unattainable ideal, making it more appealing and less intimidating.

5

"The Reason You Should Do This Is the Reason You're Hesitating" Close

By addressing the hesitation head-on, this technique encourages customers to contemplate their reasons for buying, reaffirming the value proposition and prompting a decision to move forward.

18

Mastering the C-L-O-S-E-R Framework for Effective Sales

Introduction to the C-L-O-S-E-R Framework

I n sales, having a structured approach is essential for consistently closing deals. The **C-L-O-S-E-R Framework**, inspired by Alex Hormozi's techniques, is a step-by-step guide to navigating sales calls effectively. It helps you identify client needs, address objections, and confidently close the deal. Each element of this framework plays a crucial role in ensuring that prospects move seamlessly from hesitation to commitment.

1. C - Clarify Why the Customer is There

The first step in the sales process is to **understand the customer's motivation** for reaching out. This is the foundation of any successful sales conversation. By clarifying their reasons, you set the tone for a meaningful discussion.

Objective:

Understand the prospect's motivation to open up the conversation and align your solution with their immediate concerns.

Questions to Ask:

- "What made you reach out today?"
- "What are you hoping to achieve by speaking with us?"
- "Why is this goal important to you right now?"

Purpose: Establish the client's specific needs and intentions. This not only builds rapport but also helps you tailor your pitch to their unique situation.

Action Step: Train your sales team to start every call with open-ended questions. This encourages prospects to share more information, allowing you to understand their needs deeply.

2. L - Label the Problem

Once you've clarified why the client is interested, the next step is to **identify and label their problem**. Understanding their pain points is critical because it positions your product as the solution.

Objective:

Identify and clearly define the client's pain point or problem.

Approach:

- **Label the issue**: "It sounds like you're struggling with [specific challenge]. Is that correct?"
- **Confirm the problem**: "Would you say that's your biggest hurdle right now?"

Techniques:

- Encourage the prospect to openly admit their problem.
- Use probing questions if they're unsure or hesitant. For example, "I assume you're not taking this call just for information. Is there a specific issue you're trying to resolve?"

Action Step: Role-play with your sales team to get comfortable asking deeper questions. This helps in building trust and demonstrates that you truly understand the client's challenges.

3. O - Overview Past Experiences

Understanding the client's **past efforts** to solve their problem allows you to position your solution as the best alternative. This is where you uncover what hasn't worked for them before.

Objective:

Understand what the prospect has tried before and why it didn't work.

Questions to Ask:

- "What have you tried so far to solve this problem?"
- "How long did you try that approach?"
- "What were the results?"
- "Why do you think that didn't work?"

Purpose: By having the client share their previous attempts, you highlight the gaps your solution can fill. This sets the stage for your unique value proposition.

Action Step: Use structured questioning to explore past failures. Document these responses to personalise your pitch later in the conversation.

4. S - Sell the Vacation (End Result)

Rather than focusing on the features of your product, emphasise the **end benefits** that clients will experience. This is the point where you sell the vision of what life will look like after they've used your product.

Objective:

Focus on selling the **end results** and benefits instead of the process.

Techniques:

- **Keep it brief**: Your pitch should be under 3 minutes, focusing on what the client will achieve.
- **Use vivid imagery**: For example, instead of describing the steps of a fitness program, emphasise how they'll look and feel healthier.

- **Highlight Three Key Benefits**: Example: "Our program focuses on nutrition, fitness, and accountability, ensuring comprehensive results."

Storytelling: Share relatable success stories to make the outcome tangible. For example, "Think of this like planning a vacation. You're excited about the destination, not the flight process."

  Action Step: Train your sales team to focus on the results your product delivers and use client testimonials to back up claims.

5. E - Explain Away Concerns

Objections are a natural part of the sales process. The key is to **address these concerns confidently and directly**. Common objections include price, decision-making authority, or hesitation.

Objective:

Address objections to prevent hesitation and close the sale.

Common Objections & Responses:

- **"I can't afford it."**
- Response: "If we were giving away Ferraris for $5,000, would you find a way to get the money? It's about value, not cost."
- **"I need to talk to my partner."**
- Response: "What do you think their biggest concern would be?"
- **"I need to think about it."**
- Response: Teach decision-making by breaking down what factors they should consider.

Techniques:

88

- Use the "past agreement" method: "Does your partner know you're struggling with this? Why would they oppose solving the problem?"
- Handle objections by framing them as opportunities to clarify value.

Action Step: Equip your sales team with scripts and role-playing exercises to handle objections confidently.

6. R - Reinforce the Decision

After closing the sale, it's crucial to **reinforce the client's decision** to prevent buyer's remorse and ensure a smooth onboarding process.

Objective:

Strengthen the client's confidence in their decision and set the stage for long-term satisfaction.

Techniques:

- **Send a Personalised Welcome**: Use a welcome video from the CEO or a team leader to thank the client.
- **Emphasise Their Smart Choice**: Reassure them that they've made a great decision and that your team is committed to their success.
- **Focus on the First 48 Hours**: This is the critical period where clients may second-guess their purchase.

Action Step: Standardise your follow-up process to include personalised touches like videos, welcome emails, or even a small gift to solidify the relationship.

Conclusion

The **CLOSER Framework** is a powerful tool for navigating the sales process, turning prospects into committed clients. By mastering each step—Clarifying their needs, Labelling their problems, Overviewing past experiences, Selling the end results, Explaining away objections, and Reinforcing their decision—you can close deals more effectively and ensure client satisfaction.

Key Takeaways:

1. Start by understanding the client's reasons for reaching out.
2. Dive deep into their pain points and past experiences.
3. Focus on selling the results, not just the features.
4. Address objections confidently to clear the path to a sale.
5. Reinforce the client's decision to build long-term trust.

End of Chapter Challenge: For your next sales call, follow the CLOSER Framework step-by-step. Note how it impacts your conversion rate and client satisfaction. Use the feedback to refine your approach.

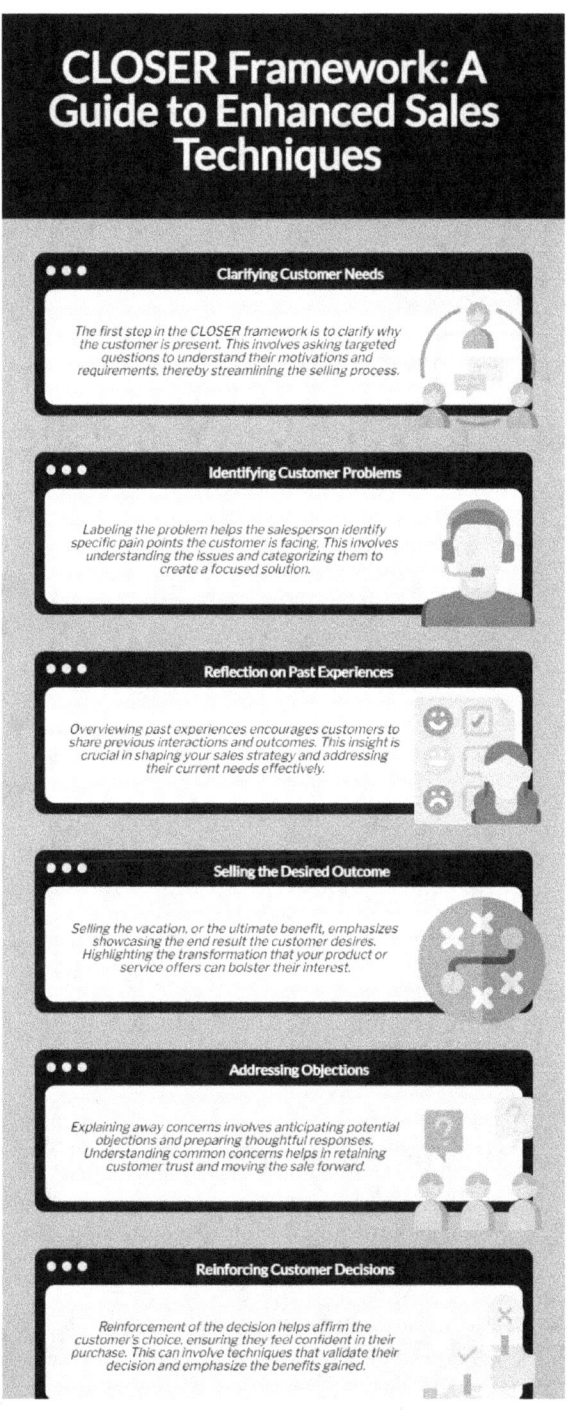

19

Mastering Sales Conversations – Simple Steps to Win Over Your Clients

I n this chapter, we'll explore how to turn a sales call into a successful conversation that builds trust, solves problems, and leads to happy clients. Imagine you're not just making a sale but genuinely helping someone improve their life or business. We'll break down these steps so even a beginner can understand. We'll also include examples from different industries to show how these strategies work in real life.

Step 1: Clarify Why the Prospect Is on the Call

Think of it like meeting a friend who's looking for advice. You wouldn't start by giving them solutions without first understanding their problem. Instead, ask, "What's going on?" This is how you should approach the beginning of a sales call.

What to Do: Ask open-ended questions like, "What challenges are you facing that you'd like help with?" This helps the person open up, and you can listen closely.

Example Scenarios:

1. **Fitness Coaching:** If you're a fitness coach, you might ask, "What's the biggest struggle you're facing in your fitness journey right now?" The client could respond, "I've tried losing weight, but nothing sticks."
2. **Digital Marketing Services:** For a business owner looking for marketing help, ask, "What's been your biggest challenge in reaching your ideal customers?" The client might share, "I'm not getting enough leads through my website."
3. **Property Management:** For a landlord seeking help with managing tenants, ask, "What's been the most challenging part of managing your properties?" They might say, "Dealing with constant maintenance requests is overwhelming."

Step 2: Deep Listening – Hearing More Than Just Words

It's important to listen to more than just what they're saying. Pay attention to how they say it—their tone of voice and choice of words can reveal a lot about their emotions and pain points.

What to Do: Pay close attention and ask follow-up questions if something seems important. For example, if they sound frustrated, ask, "Can you tell me more about why that's been so difficult?"

Example Scenarios:

1. **Fitness Coaching:** If a client says, "I've tried so many diets, but none of them work," listen to the frustration in their voice. You might respond with, "It sounds like you're really fed up with trying things that don't work."
2. **Digital Marketing:** If a business owner says, "I've spent so much

money on ads, but it feels like a waste," acknowledge that feeling. Say, "I completely understand how frustrating it must be to invest in something without seeing results."

1. **Property Management:** If a landlord says, "My tenants keep calling with issues, and it's driving me crazy," respond with empathy: "I can see how that would be exhausting."

Step 3: Future Pacing – Help Them Imagine a Better Future

Now, shift their focus from what's wrong to what could go right. Help them imagine a future where their problem is solved. This is like saying, "Imagine if everything worked out—how would that feel?"

What to Do: Ask, "If we could solve this issue, how would your life or business look in six months?" This helps the person visualise a positive change.

Example Scenarios:

1. **Fitness Coaching:** "Imagine if, in six months, you're fitting into clothes you haven't worn in years and feeling more energised every day. How would that impact your confidence?"
2. **Digital Marketing:** "Picture your business six months from now, with a steady stream of leads coming in from your website. How would that change your day-to-day operations?"
3. **Property Management:** "Imagine having all your tenant issues handled seamlessly, with maintenance requests resolved without you having to lift a finger. How much time would that free up for you?"

Step 4: Label the Prospect's Problem – Show Them You Understand

People want to feel understood. By repeating back what they've told you in their own words, you show that you're truly listening.

What to Do: Restate their pain points back to them. For example, "It sounds like you've been struggling to manage your tenants effectively, and it's really eating up your time. Is that right?"

Example Scenarios:

1. **Fitness Coaching:** "It sounds like you've been trying different workouts and diets, but nothing seems to stick. That must be really discouraging."
2. **Digital Marketing:** "I hear that you've tried running ads, but they haven't brought the results you were hoping for. That can be really frustrating."
3. **Property Management:** "It sounds like maintenance issues are taking up more of your time than you'd like, and it's preventing you from focusing on other important tasks."

Step 5: Review Their Past Attempts – What Didn't Work and Why

Before jumping to your solution, explore what they've tried before and why it didn't work. This shows that you understand their problem better than anyone else.

What to Do: Ask, "What have you tried before? Why do you think it didn't work?" Then explain why your approach is different.

Example Scenarios:

1. **Fitness Coaching:** "You've tried quick-fix diets, but they just led to yo-yo dieting. Our program focuses on sustainable changes, so you won't feel like you're on a diet at all."
2. **Digital Marketing:** "You've invested in ads, but without targeting the right audience, it's like throwing money into the wind. Our strategy focuses on reaching the exact people who need your product."
3. **Property Management:** "You've been handling maintenance calls yourself, but that's not scalable. We have a system that takes care of all that, so you can focus on growing your portfolio."

Step 6: Sell the Vacation, Not the Plane Flight

When selling, don't get caught up in listing features. Instead, paint a picture of what life will look like once they've achieved their goal. Focus on the benefits.

What to Do: Use emotional storytelling to show the transformation they'll experience.

Example Scenarios:

1. **Fitness Coaching:** "Imagine waking up every morning feeling fit, healthy, and full of energy. That's what our program will help you achieve."
2. **Digital Marketing:** "Think about the joy of seeing your business thrive, with customers reaching out to you instead of you chasing them."
3. **Property Management:** "Picture having happy tenants and a stress-free property management process, allowing you to focus on expanding your investments."

Step 7: Address Concerns Early – Overcome Objections Before They Come Up

People will always have concerns, but if you address them early on, you can prevent them from becoming roadblocks.

What to Do: Proactively discuss common objections like cost, time, and commitment. For example, "A lot of clients worry about the cost, but the results speak for themselves."

Example Scenarios:

1. **Fitness Coaching:** "You might wonder if this is worth the investment, but imagine the health benefits you'll gain that no amount of money can buy."
2. **Digital Marketing:** "I understand that marketing feels risky, but the ROI we've achieved for other clients speaks for itself."
3. **Property Management:** "Managing properties yourself can seem like saving money, but the time and stress it saves are priceless."

Step 8: Reinforce Their Decision – Celebrate Their Choice

Once they've agreed to work with you, make them feel great about their decision. Follow up with a personal touch.

What to Do: Send a quick thank-you video or message after the call. Then, create a 30-day plan to ensure they see quick wins.

Example Scenarios:

1. **Fitness Coaching:** "I'm so excited for you to start your fitness journey with us. I'll check in next week to see how you're feeling after your first workout."
2. **Digital Marketing:** "Thank you for trusting us to handle your marketing. I'll reach out in a week with the first set of results."
3. **Property Management:** "Welcome aboard! I'll touch base next week to review how we're handling your first set of tenant requests."

Summary: The Path to Sales Success

By using these strategies, you can turn a sales call into a meaningful conversation. Here's a quick recap:

1. **Understand their challenges** through thoughtful questions.
2. **Listen deeply** to their concerns.
3. **Paint a picture** of a better future.
4. **Show how your solution** is different and valuable.
5. **Celebrate their decision** to work with you.

By mastering these steps, you'll not only close more sales but also build lasting relationships with your clients. That's the key to becoming a true sales master!

End-of-Chapter Checklist

1. Did you ask enough open-ended questions to understand their challenges?
2. Did you listen carefully and restate their problems to show empathy?
3. Did you help them imagine a better future?
4. Did you address any concerns before they became roadblocks?
5. Did you celebrate their decision to work with you?

Action Step for the Reader

- Choose a potential client you've been talking to. Try using the steps from this chapter to turn your next sales call into a successful conversation.

20

The Power of Reframing – Turning Objections into Opportunities- 3A Framework-How to keep control of conversation

Introduction

In sales, asking questions is a powerful way to stay in control of the conversation. The idea is simple: the person who asks the questions is the one steering where the conversation goes. Instead of just answering the prospect's questions directly—which might lead to losing control—the salesperson can respond by reframing those questions and asking follow-up questions. This way, the salesperson keeps the conversation on track, addresses any concerns, and guides it toward a positive outcome, making it more likely to close the sale successfully.

Imagine you're trying to convince someone to try something new, but they keep bringing up concerns and questions. This can happen in sales calls all the time. The best salespeople, like Alex Hormozi, know that instead of getting frustrated, losing control of conversation and turning into a defensive position , how to use these objections as opportunities and keep control of conversation to build trust and close the deal.

How? The secret lies in a powerful technique called **3A reframing**. Reframing means taking a prospect's question or concern and turning it around to show them a new perspective—one that makes them excited about saying "yes" to your offer. In this chapter, we'll explore how to use the **3A Framework** to reframe objections in a way that's easy to understand and apply in any sales situation. The 3A Framework stands for:

1. **Acknowledge** the concern.
2. **Associate** it with a positive outcome.
3. **Ask** a follow-up question to keep the conversation moving forward.

Think of it like this: if someone is standing in front of a door that's locked, instead of trying to convince them to force it open, you simply show them another door that's already open. By using this approach, you can turn even the most sceptical prospects into happy clients.

We'll use the **3A Framework (Acknowledge, Associate, Ask)** to turn potentially "trap" questions into opportunities for deeper conversations. Here's how to reframe some common types of questions to maintain control and guide the prospect towards seeing the real value of your service.

-How to Handle Certification Concerns Using Reframing

When a prospect asks, "How many certifications do your trainers have?" It can be a tricky question. Rather than directly answering, which may not satisfy the prospect, use **reframing** to redirect the conversation. Here's how:

1. **Acknowledge** the Question:

- **Example:** "That's a great question. I understand that certifications can be important to some people."

1. **Reframe by Asking a Clarifying Question:**

- Instead of directly stating the number of certifications (which they may judge as insufficient or irrelevant), turn it into a conversation to uncover what's really important to them.
- **Example Question:** "Which specific certifications are you looking for? Are there certain skills or results you're hoping to achieve through those certifications?"

1. **Guide the Conversation Toward Value:**

- The goal is to shift the focus from certifications to the actual outcomes and results your service or product can deliver.
- **Follow-Up Question:** "What's most important to you—having certified trainers or achieving your fitness goals faster than you thought possible?"

Key Takeaway:

The person asking the questions is in control. By reframing a certification concern into a deeper conversation about results and value, you take charge of the dialogue, building trust and guiding the prospect to see what truly matters.

-How to Handle Spouse-Related Concerns

When a prospect says, "I need to talk to my spouse before making a decision," it can be challenging because they might use this as a reason to delay or avoid making a commitment. Here's how to reframe it:

1. **Acknowledge** the Concern:

- **Example:** "I completely understand—it's important to make sure your spouse is on board with big decisions."

1. **Reframe by Asking a Clarifying Question:**

- Instead of just accepting this as a final answer, ask questions to understand their true concern.
- **Example Question:** "What specific questions or concerns do you think your spouse might have about this? I'd be happy to address them so you're fully prepared for that conversation."

1. **Guide the Conversation Toward Value:**

- Shift the focus to how your product or service benefits both of them.
- **Follow-Up Question:** "If your spouse knew that this could help you [achieve a specific benefit], do you think they'd be supportive?"

Key Takeaway:

By reframing the spouse's concern, you stay in control and uncover whether the prospect has any hidden objections of their own. This approach also helps you equip them with the information needed to discuss it with their partner confidently.

-How to Handle Cost-Related Concerns

When a prospect says, "This is too expensive" or "I can't afford it right now," it's often a sign that they haven't yet seen the full value of what you're offering. Here's how to reframe it:

1. **Acknowledge** the Concern:

- **Example:** "I completely understand—budget is definitely something to consider."

1. **Reframe by Asking a Clarifying Question:**

- Instead of defending your pricing right away, dig deeper to understand their hesitation.
- **Example Question:** "When you say it's expensive, do you mean it's outside of your budget right now, or are you concerned about the return on investment?"

1. **Guide the Conversation Toward Value:**

- Focus on the benefits and results they'll gain from your service, rather than just the cost.
- **Follow-Up Question:** "If you could start seeing results in just a few weeks, would that make this investment feel more worthwhile? What would achieving [specific goal] be worth to you?"

Key Takeaway:
By reframing cost concerns, you shift the conversation from price to value. This helps prospects see the investment in terms of the results they'll achieve, making them more likely to commit.

Below, we'll go through some more **10 examples** across different industries to show you how this technique works in real life. Each example is simple and clear so that anyone can understand how to use the 3A Framework effectively.

Example 1: Personal Training Program

Prospect: "How many certifications do your trainers have?"

1. **Acknowledge:** "I understand that certifications can be really important to some people."
2. **Associate:** "However, we've found that real-world results and experience often matter more than just certificates on paper. Our trainers focus on getting you the results you want."
3. **Ask:** "What specific certifications are you looking for, and how do you see them contributing to the results you're hoping to achieve?"

Example 2: Online Marketing Course

Prospect: "Is your course certified by any official organisations?"

1. **Acknowledge:** "That's a great question. Certifications can be reassuring for many people."
2. **Associate:** "However, the entrepreneurs who've taken our course have seen significant growth in their businesses because we focus on practical, actionable strategies rather than just theoretical certifications."
3. **Ask:** "What type of certification are you looking for, and how would it impact your decision to grow your business with our course?"

Example 3: Corporate Training Program

Prospect: "What certifications do your instructors hold?"

1. **Acknowledge:** "I completely understand why you'd want to know that."
2. **Associate:** "While some trainers focus solely on certifications, our team emphasises hands-on experience in solving real business challenges. That's where we see the biggest impact."
3. **Ask:** "Is there a particular certification you're interested in, or are you more focused on the outcomes our training can achieve for your team?"

Example 4: Health Coaching Service

Prospect: "Do your coaches have certifications in nutrition?"

1. **Acknowledge:** "I hear you—having certified experts can give peace of mind."
2. **Associate:** "Our coaches are experienced in creating customised plans that get real results. Many of our clients have seen transformations that no certificate alone could achieve."
3. **Ask:** "Which specific nutrition certification are you looking for, and how would that affect your confidence in starting your health journey with us?"

Example 5: Digital Marketing Agency

Prospect: "How many certifications do your SEO specialists have?"

1. **Acknowledge:** "I understand certifications can be seen as a mark of expertise."
2. **Associate:** "In our experience, what really counts is the ability to deliver consistent results. Our specialists have helped dozens of businesses rank on the first page of Google, regardless of certifications."
3. **Ask:** "What specific certification do you feel is most important for SEO, and what would it mean for your business's growth?"

Example 6: Online Coding Bootcamp

Prospect: "Is your program certified by any tech organisations?"

1. **Acknowledge:** "I see why that's an important consideration for you."
2. **Associate:** "While we don't have an official certification, our graduates have landed jobs at top tech firms because we teach them the real-world skills employers are looking for."
3. **Ask:** "What certification would be most valuable to you, and are you more focused on landing a job after completing the course?"

Example 7: Personal Development Coaching

Prospect: "Are your coaches certified life coaches?"

1. **Acknowledge:** "That's a fair question—certifications can sometimes indicate a level of training."
2. **Associate:** "Our focus is on delivering life-changing results through years of practical experience rather than relying solely on certifications."
3. **Ask:** "Which certification would you consider most important, and how would it impact your confidence in achieving your personal goals with us?"

Example 8: Property Management Service

Prospect: "Do your property managers hold industry certifications?"

1. **Acknowledge:** "I completely understand why certifications would matter when entrusting someone with your property."
2. **Associate:** "What sets us apart is our track record of increasing rental income and reducing tenant turnover, thanks to years of hands-on management experience."
3. **Ask:** "Is there a particular certification that's important to you, or are you more interested in the results we can deliver?"

Example 9: Language Learning Platform

Prospect: "Is your language course certified by educational boards?"

1. **Acknowledge:** "That's a valid concern—certifications can sometimes provide reassurance."
2. **Associate:** "Instead of focusing on certificates, we prioritise immersive, practical learning that leads to fluency much faster than traditional courses."
3. **Ask:** "Would an official certification be more important to you, or would becoming fluent in the language in six months be a better outcome?"

Example 10: Business Coaching Program

Prospect: "Are your business coaches certified?"

1. **Acknowledge:** "I can see why you'd ask that—certifications can be one way to judge expertise."
2. **Associate:** "However, our clients have found the real value in the results we've helped them achieve, from scaling their revenue to streamlining operations."
3. **Ask:** "What certification would make you feel more confident, and are you more interested in seeing a tangible increase in your business growth?"

In these examples, you're not just answering the question; you're redirecting the conversation to uncover the prospect's real concerns. This way, you stay in control of the conversation while addressing their underlying needs and demonstrating the value of your service.

These reframing techniques allow you to maintain control of the conversation, uncover hidden objections, and guide the prospect toward making a confident decision.

Pro Tip

There are four important rules for using reframing in an ethical way.

First, you must genuinely believe in the product or service you're offering; this ensures you're always acting in the best interest of the prospect.

Second, avoid asking, "Do you have any questions?" because it can make the conversation feel abrupt and may put the prospect on the spot.

Third, never disagree with the prospect directly, as this can create unnecessary tension. Instead, use techniques like "straw men" or foils—introducing a hypothetical concern that you can address—to tackle tough topics without confrontation.

Finally, approach every conversation with a childlike curiosity. This helps you stay open, ask meaningful questions, and understand the prospect's true needs, which leads to a more genuine and effective sales process.

EXAMPLE

Prospect: "I'm not sure if your coaching program will actually help me grow my business. I've tried other coaches, and they didn't work."

Step 1: Believe in Your Product

- **Internal Mindset:** You genuinely know that your coaching program has helped many businesses grow and that it provides real, actionable value.

Step 2: Avoid Asking "Do You Have Any Questions?"

- Instead of saying, "Do you have any questions?" (which might lead to the prospect focusing on doubts), you can respond with curiosity to understand their concerns better.

Reframing with the 3A Framework:

1. **Acknowledge:**

- "I completely understand where you're coming from. It can be frustrating to invest in something and not see the results you expected."

1. **Associate (Using a Straw Man):**

- "A lot of our clients came to us feeling exactly the same way. They had tried other coaches before, but the reason they didn't see results was often because those coaches focused only on theory rather than giving practical, step-by-step strategies."

(Here, the "straw man" is the idea of other coaches being too theoretical. By presenting it this way, you're addressing a tough truth indirectly without disagreeing with the prospect.)

1. **Ask (Retaining Childlike Curiosity):**

- "Out of curiosity, what specific results were you hoping to achieve with those other coaches that didn't quite work out? And what would you consider a big win if you could achieve it within the next three months?"

Why This Works:

- **You maintain trust** by agreeing with the prospect's feelings rather than dismissing their concerns.
- **Using the straw man technique**, you indirectly highlight how your service is different without directly criticising the competition.
- By showing **genuine curiosity**, you encourage the prospect to open up about their true needs, which helps you position your solution as the best fit.

This approach keeps the conversation positive and constructive, ultimately guiding the prospect toward seeing how your coaching program is exactly what they need.

21

Mastering the Art of Questions to Close More Sales

Introduction: The Power of Asking the Right Questions

I magine you're trying to help a friend decide which toy they should buy. Instead of just telling them what to get, you ask questions like, "What do you want to play with?" or "What's your favourite kind of game?" That way, they figure out what they really want, and it feels like their own decision.

In sales, it works the same way. By asking good questions, you guide people to see their own problems and realise that your product or service can solve them. The key is to make them feel like they're discovering the solution on their own.

Quick Story:

- Let's say you're trying to sell a soccer ball to someone. Instead of saying, "This is the best ball ever," you ask, "What's the biggest problem you have with your current ball?" Maybe they say it doesn't last long. Then you can show them how your ball is more durable and better for their games.

Section 1: The Magic of Asking Questions

Why Ask Questions?

- Questions are powerful because they help people think about their problems and realise why they need a solution. It's like being a detective, finding out what the person really needs before showing them how you can help.

Examples of Good Questions to Ask:

1. "What are you struggling with?"

- This helps the person think about their challenges.

1. "What have you tried so far? How's that working for you?"

- This gets them to see that what they've done hasn't worked, so they're open to something new.

1. "Why is this important to you?"

- Now you're getting them to think about why solving this problem matters.

Practical Scenario:

- Imagine you're talking to someone who wants to lose weight. Instead of saying, "You should try my fitness program," ask them:
- "What's been the hardest part about losing weight for you?"
- "What have you tried so far? Did it give you the results you wanted?"
- "Why is getting fit important to you?"

By asking these questions, they'll realise their old methods haven't worked, and they might be more interested in hearing about your program.

Activity:

- Practice writing down three questions you can ask someone who might be interested in what you're selling. Make sure the questions help them think about their problems.

Section 2: Restate and Clarify to Build Trust

Why Restating Matters

- When you repeat what someone says, it shows you're really listening. People like to feel heard, and when they do, they trust you more.

How to Restate What They Say:

- Use phrases like:
- "So what I'm hearing is that the main issue is…"
- "It sounds like you've tried X, Y, and Z but haven't seen the results you wanted. Is that correct?"
- This way, you make sure you understand them, and they feel understood.

Real-Life Example:

- Let's say you're talking to a parent who's worried about their child's grades. They tell you they've tried different tutors, but nothing seems to work. You can say:

- "So, it sounds like you've already tried tutoring, but it hasn't helped improve their grades. Is that right?"
- This shows you're listening and helps them feel like you really understand their problem.

Activity:

- Think of a time when you were talking to someone, and they didn't seem to understand you. Write down how you could have used a phrase like, "So what I'm hearing is…" to show you were listening better.

Section 3: Using Stories and Analogies to Break Beliefs

Why Stories Are Powerful

- Stories help people imagine themselves solving their problems. It's easier to understand something through a story than through complicated explanations.

Example of a Story:

- If you're trying to sell a fitness program, instead of saying, "This program will work," tell them a story:
- "Imagine you're trying to lose weight but keep failing because diets are too strict. It's like trying to ride a bike uphill without any gears—it's exhausting! What if I told you there's a way to reach your goal without giving up all your favourite foods?"

Using Analogies:

- An analogy is like a comparison. For example:
- "Trying to get fit without the right guidance is like trying to build a house without a blueprint. It's possible, but it's way harder."

Activity:

- Write a short story or analogy that you can use to help someone understand why they need your product or service.

Section 4: Tips for Closing Without Pushing

When to Pitch Your Solution

- Don't start talking about your product or service until the person is already convinced that they have a problem and they need help. The idea is to let them figure out they want your help first.

How to Know When They're Ready:

1. They start asking you questions about how your product works.
2. They're nodding along and agreeing with you.
3. They say things like, "I really need something like this."

Quick Tips:

- Keep the conversation focused on their problems, not on your product.
- If they're still unsure, ask more questions to help them see why they need

help.

Example:

- If someone says, "I don't know if I have time to start a fitness program," you could ask, "Do you think you'll have more time next year, or will things always be busy?" This helps them realise that waiting won't solve their problem.

Conclusion: Guiding Prospects to Their Own Decisions

Sales isn't about pushing someone to buy something they don't want. It's about helping them see why they need your help and letting them decide for themselves. When you ask good questions, listen carefully, and use stories, people will feel like they're making the best choice on their own.

Final Thought: "The best salespeople don't sell—they guide people to their own decisions."

End-of-Chapter Checklist

1. Did you ask enough questions to understand the person's problem?
2. Did you restate what they said to show you were listening?
3. Did you use a story or analogy to explain how your solution can help?
4. Did you wait until they were ready before pitching your solution?

Action Step for the Reader

- Think about someone who might need your product or service. Write down three questions you could ask them to understand their problem better. Then, think of a story you can share to help them see why your solution works.

22

Conclusion

Your Path to Sales Mastery

Congratulations on making it to the end of **"Sales Mastery: Practical Techniques to Close Deals Like Alex Hormozi"**! By now, you've absorbed a wealth of techniques, strategies, and frameworks designed to elevate your sales game to the next level.

But remember, the journey doesn't end here. **Sales mastery isn't achieved by simply reading a book**—it's about applying what you've learned consistently, refining your approach, and continuously learning from each interaction.

Here are a few parting thoughts to guide you:

1. **Start Small, But Start Now**: Don't wait for the perfect moment to put these techniques into practice. Start small, test what you've learned, and gradually refine your approach. **The sooner you act, the faster you'll see results**.

2. **Embrace the Process**: Sales is a skill that requires practice and patience. You will face rejection, objections, and challenges. That's part of

the game. But with the tools you've gained here—like the **CLOSER Framework** and objection-handling techniques—you're well-equipped to navigate these hurdles.

3. **Focus on Relationships, Not Just Transactions**: The best salespeople are those who prioritise relationships over quick wins. Focus on understanding your clients, meeting their needs, and building trust. A satisfied client today can become a loyal advocate tomorrow.

Call to Action: Put Your Skills to the Test

- **Challenge Yourself**: Use the techniques from this book to set a new personal sales goal. Whether it's closing more high-ticket deals, overcoming specific objections, or simply boosting your conversion rate—commit to applying at least one technique you've learned.
- **Reflect and Adjust**: After each sales interaction, take a moment to reflect. What went well? Where did you stumble? Keep refining your approach using the frameworks and techniques you've learned here.
- **Join the Community**: If you're serious about continuous growth, consider joining a sales community or mastermind group where you can share experiences, get feedback, and learn from others who are on the same journey.

A Final Word

Mastering sales is more than just closing deals—it's about becoming a trusted advisor, building long-term relationships, and truly helping clients achieve their goals. The journey may not always be easy, but it is incredibly rewarding. Thank you for investing your time in this book. Now, it's your turn to take what you've learned and transform it into real-world results. Go out there, close those deals, and remember: the world needs what you're selling—**it's your job to show them why**.

Looking Ahead: This is Just the Beginning

You've reached the end of **Volume One** of "Sales Mastery: Practical Techniques to Close Deals Like Alex Hormozi." But remember, this is just the start of your journey toward becoming a sales expert. The strategies and frameworks you've learned here are the foundation, and there's so much more to explore. In the upcoming volumes, we'll dive even deeper into advanced sales techniques, mindset shifts, and powerful tools that will further transform how you approach every sales conversation. Stay tuned for the next volume, where we'll uncover new ways to elevate your skills, overcome even greater challenges, and continue your journey to sales mastery. Until then, keep practising, keep learning, and most importantly—keep closing.

www.ingramcontent.com/pod-product-compliance
Lightning Source LLC
Chambersburg PA
CBHW071516220526
45472CB00003B/1048